MW00777759

Smoke
And
Fire

Steaming Through Smoke and Fire

1871

True Stories of Shipwreck and Disaster On The Great Lakes

By James L. Donahue

New Printing by Thunder Bay Press
Holt, Michigan

Library of Congress Catalog Card Number: 90-93084

International Standard Book Number: 0-9626947-0-3

First Edition 1990
Second Edition 1995

About the Title

The title of this book, Steaming Through Smoke and Fire 1871, reflects the historic fires that swept Chicago, Pestigo, Wis., and the forests across Michigan, Wisconsin, Minnesota and northern Ohio. Many small communities and many lives were lost during the first week of October 1871. Several fine ships burned in port and others were wrecked because of the heavy smoke that blinded sailors on the lakes.

About the Cover Art

The pen and ink drawing on the cover and face page was prepared by St. Clair, Michigan, artist Pamela A. Clary. It is one of two of Clary's works that appear in this book. The cover picture was taken from a photograph of the Detroit and Cleveland sidewheeler *State of New York* while docked at Port Sanilac, Michigan, at about 1911. The boat was built as the *City of Mackinac* in 1883 and is an example of the type of steamboat on the lakes during the period.

This book is dedicated to Doris, who
puts up with my passion for exploring
the cobwebs of the past.

Table of Contents

Special thanks to the following people who helped me research the information in this book, then learn the many tricks of becoming a publisher. Robert W. Graham, archivist, and Jay Martin, assistant archivist; Dr. Stuart R. Givens, former acting director; Joan Sleda, former curator; Susan Riggs, secretary, all at the Institute for Great Lakes Research, Perrysburg, Ohio; Harriet Eagle, head librarian, and her assistants, Sharron Merritt and Jackie Graves, Sandusky Public Library; James Ketchum, James and Pat Stayer; David Fritz, the Rev. Peter Van der Linden, plus many unknown librarians in towns bordering the lakes who assisted in a variety of ways.

The Illustrations came from various sources. Most of the photographs were found in the files at the Institute for Great Lakes Research, Perrysburg, Ohio. Photos of the R. G. Coburn, Forest Queen and George B. McClellan were obtained from the Milwaukee Public Library. The painting of the Novarino was done by the Rev. Edward Dowling, Detroit. The cover drawing and drawing of the bark Mary E. Perew are by artist Pamela A. Clary, St. Clair, Mich. Proper acknowledgements appear elsewhere.

Introduction

When we were children growing up at Harbor Beach, Michigan, along the rocky coast of Lake Huron, none of us dreamed that there was a graveyard of sunken ships lying within a few hundred feet of our daily playground.

The first hint that disasters of that magnitude ever happened came one dry summer when lake water levels dropped lower than normal and we saw the ribs of a sunken schooner exposed near the south end of the harbor breakwall. With each trip to the beach, more and more of the wreck appeared. The skeleton of an ancient horror was rising from its watery grave, an obscene reminder of the frailties of both men and their machines. It silently spoke of death and despair. . . of lost men, lost cargo and lost dreams.

I spent a lot of time looking at the wreck, wondering when and how it happened; asking questions. The adults around me didn't know any more about the skeletal remains than I, and their answers to my constant questions were the vague, uncommitted kind that grown-ups so often use with children. I think that may have been the beginning of my personal quest for knowledge about the past. Now, years later, I have returned to the area as a writer, still wanting to know and understand the things that happened on the lakes during an earlier era. We are only now discovering that old hulk to be one of thousands of ships left ruined a century ago on the jagged coasts that surround the Great Lakes.

The wrecks have been exposed by modern technology which has led to such wonderful inventions as portable sonar and scuba diving equipment. Now sport divers and marine archaeologists can use relatively inexpensive electronic probing devices from the decks of pleasure boats to locate wrecks, then use safe diving equipment complete with portable air packs to drop down on them and explore with ease. As more and more of the forgotten relics are found, marked and identified, it is to our surprise that we are discovering the lake bottoms to be a literal graveyard of ships.

This book is a collection of stories about nearly all of the vessels that were lost between Duluth and Quebec, from

Oswego to Chicago, during the year 1871. And it is much more. It attempts to take a slice out of Great Lakes history and paint a broad view of what was happening during the dynamic years after the Civil War. The stories are exciting tales about the hundreds of disasters and near-disasters that happened in one year. They also look into the way politics of the period affected shipping, the lumber empire, the movement to open a way for larger ships and heavier cargoes, and, whenever possible, examine the living conditions, and, unfortunately, the dying conditions for the sailors.

I chose the year 1871 because it was an exciting time of growth and development in North America. We were a restless people in a young nation, having just survived a great war within our own borders. Now we were devoting our time to claiming the great forests, prairies and western mountains of a vast land that seemed to have no end. We were armed then with many new tools developed from the necessities of war. New and larger iron clad ships were powered by improved engines. Faster propeller driven ships were proving themselves to be superior to vessels moved by side wheels. As popular as they were in 1871, the steamboats hadn't crowded out the sailing ships. Not only were the horizons black with a constant spewing of coal smoke, but the scene was cheered by a spate of sails from schooners, barkentines, and a variety of other types of sailing boats all running before the wind.

The boats came in all shapes and sizes in 1871. While the tall ships were still operating on their own, many schooners, barks and scows were converted for use as tow barges. The more efficient steam powered ships often had a string of barges in tow with each trip up and down the lakes. The other vessels to be seen were side wheel steamers, propellers, steam barges (commonly called freighters today), and tugs. The steam boats usually were designed to carry passengers and freight at the same time. The tugs did exactly what their name said they did. They were small vessels with powerful engines that pulled great log rafts, or strings of barges loaded with cargo up and down the lakes. Other tugs were used to assist sailing ships enter and leave the confines of the many harbors, salvaging sunken and grounded ships, and towing sailing ships up and down the St. Clair and Detroit Rivers. They were the workhorse of the lakes. These types of ships jammed the lakes each season from about mid-April, when the ice melted, until early December, when the ice returned. The boats on the Great Lakes were so many in number that they seemed to create traffic jams in the various ports. One Michigan newspaper editor wrote that he could count no less than ten vessels on the horizon off his shoreline community as he looked out of his window.

It was during those busy months that the sailors ran their ships into reefs, or hit bottom in the shallow offshore waters. The wooden vessels burned, exploded and sometimes their cranky engines just fell apart. They collided with each other, collided with breakwalls, and sometimes dashed themselves against docks and bridges. Many sailed off into eternity. They sank, leaving no trace and no survivors to tell what happened. Some sailors referred to that type of disappearance as "falling through the crack." Each sinking was a disaster. Sailors drowned. Ships, which had a special personality of their own to the men who served on them, were lost forever. Millions of dollars in cargo never reached its destination.

This book is directed to all of the people who look at ribs of old ships in the water and want to know why. May their questions always be answered.

The schooner *Tasmania,* launched in 1871 as the *James Couch,* was among the first of the four masted sailing ships built on the lakes.

The Way It Was

Everything was ready.

A hush fell over the crowd that chilly spring Saturday afternoon, April 22, 1871, as sweaty workers swung heavy steel hammers to knock the last blocks away. Slowly the mammoth hulk towering above the people began to move. The ground rumbled from the weight as the monster ship, christened the *James Couch*, slid sideways down a heavy wooden track until it hit the silt-stained water of the Black River at Port Huron, Michigan, with a mighty splash. The hull rocked violently in the water for a few dramatic moments. Everybody watched as the few daring souls who rode on its decks to the water gripped the rail and enjoyed the sensation of a modern carnival ride. People began to cheer. Gentlemen tossed their hats into the sky as the success of another launch set a festive attitude. At Port Huron, a launching was always a gala occasion but this one marked a milestone for the industry.

The *Couch*, a schooner named for a prominent Chicago businessman of the day, was one of the first of a new line of big ships built that year. Among the first four masted sailing ships launched on the lakes, the *Couch* was destined to set new records in the volume of grain shipped from Chicago east to Buffalo. While large in comparison to other vessels of the day, the new boat measured just two hundred ten feet long . . . a mere midget compared to the monster thousand-foot ships plying the Great Lakes today. Even so, it signaled a new interest in increased commerce, one that called for major government construction projects opening new and larger locks and channels connecting the lakes with each other, and with the outside world.

It was an era of exciting change. The nation was going through reconstruction following the Civil War. The people were still recovering from the shock of both the war and the assassination of President Abraham Lincoln. The nation's newest war hero, General Ulysses S. Grant, was in the White House. His held the presidency from 1869 to 1877.

The invention of the steam engine and newly developed process for making steel were streamlining the industrial revolution. Steam engines were running trains, ships, tractors and industry. It was a time of rapid change. Workers were learning to use new industrial tools to create other work saving inventions such as the threshing and sewing machines. Alexander Graham Bell introduced the telephone to the world in 1877, and Thomas Edison gave us the first practical electric light bulb in 1879.

All was not progress, however. The year 1871 fell during a period of exploitation of the southern states by the carpetbaggers, the creation of America's first terrorist organization, the Klu Klux Klan, and the national shame of political corruption by men like Tammany leader "Boss" Tweed, who pilfered millions of dollars out of the New York City treasury. The great Chicago fire plus the burning of thousands of acres of forests and smaller towns in Wisconsin, Minnesota and Michigan occurred during the fall of 1871. Another devastating fire destroyed the City of Boston the following year. It was thought that the fires contributed to the panic of 1873 that brought the nation's business to a stand still.

Newspapers began springing up in more and more places. They became outlets for leading writers and humorists of the period. Among the best were Mark Twain, Josh Billings, Petroleum V. Nasby and Horatio Alger Jr.

It also was a time of the settlement of the west and all of the characters of western lore were in place. The ranchers and cowboys were on the job, punching cows and bringing them on long cattle drives to railroad centers for marketing. People were still searching for that elusive California gold. The western outlaws were building legends. A few hundred Native Americans were still roaming free, although they were being hunted shamelessly by the U. S. Army. General George A. Custer took his last stand at the Little Big Horn River, Montana, on June 25, 1876.

America celebrated its first century in grand style in 1876. A Centennial Exhibition was established that year at Philadelphia to mark the occasion. The United States by then had thirty-eight states so there were thirty-eight stars on the flag. The population was measured at some forty to fifty million people. The nation was already known as the world's greatest producer of food and as a growing industrial power.

All of this was having a big influence on the shipping industry on the Great Lakes. The boats were hauling grain from the midwest, iron ore and copper from the mines in northern Michigan and Minnesota, coal and steel from Ohio and New York, and lumber from the forests of Michigan, Wisconsin and Ontario to all parts of the fast growing nation. They also were a primary means of transportation for settlers moving across the country, looking for new land in the west. Before the railroads were finished, people used the lakes to travel from Kingston to Buffalo, Toledo, Detroit, Chicago and ports in between.

The construction of the canals and locks at Welland and Sault Ste. Marie in the 1850s opened all of the lakes as one great thoroughfare. The Erie Canal across New York to Buffalo became the final link for lake commerce between Duluth, Chicago, Detroit and New York. From New York, all of the ports of Europe became fair game for business ventures in the United States.

The decision by Congress to create the U. S. Weather Bureau in 1870 would play an important role in protecting shipping. Electronic communication devices were quickly appearing on the scene. Telegraph lines were strung along much of the coastline, and the telephone arrived less than a decade later. Sailors soon were going to have something more to warn them about approaching storms than their knowledge of barometric pressure and clouds, and their own sixth sense. Edison's electric light bulb was not marketed until the end of this period. When it came, it improved safety aboard ships. Not only could these new lights be seen better at night, but vessels could be lighted without the danger of fire from kerosene and oil lamps.

Michigan was the home of the great lumber barons in the 1870s. They owned large tracts of white pine, tamarack and hardwoods, and were turning towns such as Bay City, Cheboygan and South Haven into big lumber centers for the midwest. As the trees were cleared, the rich land began supplying an abundant amount of grain. The lakes were found to be filled with fish, spawning a great fishing industry. Copper and iron ore were mined along the Lake Superior coast, and hauled to refineries at places like Gary, Detroit, Cleveland, Erie and Buffalo.

Roads were primitive in 1871, and railroads were still to be constructed through the wilderness of northern Michigan, Wisconsin and Ontario. Thus boats remained the main mode of travel. Most vessels were carrying both passengers and freight in 1871, which meant additional lives in peril whenever vessels were wrecked.

And wreck they did . . .

SPRING

Burning Of The *Florence*

On the Detroit River,
Amherstburg, Ont.,
Saturday, March 4

Harsh winter winds were still whipping the lakes the night flames broke out aboard the iron hulled steamship *Florence*. Perhaps it was a defective flue from the watchman's coal stove, or carelessly dumped ash from his pipe that caused the fire. The cause lies obscured now by the dull grayness of time. There was no newspaper to record the story in the river town of Amherstburg, where the steamer was docked. Anyone who would have known what happened has long passed on.

The volunteer fire fighters of Amherstburg were summoned to the docks at 11:00 PM when smoke and flames were seen pouring out of the wooden cabin windows and doors on the main deck. The fire got hot enough to melt the ice still draped over the ship's iron hull. When the fire was out, much of the superstructure of the package freight and passenger hauler was a charred ruin. The fire did not destroy the *Florence*, however. The boat remained afloat and its engine was intact. Nobody was hurt.

The steamer was one of two small vessels owned by S. and H. Jenkins of Amherstburg and serving Canadian ports up and down the Detroit and St. Clair Rivers. The fire couldn't have happened at a worse time for the Jenkins. The warming sun of spring was quickly breaking up the ice in the rivers and a few vessels were already getting up steam for short trips. The shipping season was almost started. The other vessel on Jenkins' line, the *Essex*, was also out of commission that month. The *Essex* was laid up for extensive refurbishing and was not expected back in service for a few more weeks. Thus it was that when the shipping season officially opened, the Jenkins were forced to lease a third vessel, identified as the *Favorite,* to fill the gap.

The *Florence* was rebuilt and remained on the water until it was dismantled in 1922. The ship originally measured forty-two feet, six inches in length, and nine feet, three inches wide at the beam when built at Baltimore in 1869. It was rebuilt at Grand Haven in 1888 and lengthened to seventy-one feet, and widened to fourteen feet.

Lost Fishermen

On Lake Michigan,
Near St. Joseph, Mich.
Monday, March 27

Fishermen are among the pluckiest sailors. They go to sea in all types of weather in small craft because they depend on their trade to live.

The long winter months on the Great Lakes are hard on fishermen because when they can't catch fish, their income stops. They consequently are known to brave ice floes and terrible early and late winter storms to get the last haul of fish each fall, and man the first vessels out of the harbor in the spring. Their eagerness sometimes costs them their lives.

This is what happened to the four fishermen who braved rough weather on Lake Michigan on the schooner *Emma* on March 27. Their vessel capsized and all four men, identified as Charles Ott, Peter Broderick, Jacob Kissinger and John Meicher, were drowned. The accident happened ten miles southwest of St. Joseph, at about 2:00 PM.

The steamer *Marine City* worried its owners when it spent a week stuck in the ice at Cheboygan.

Battling Ice

Shipping on the Great Lakes has always been controlled by the seasons. The boats stop moving during the winter because they can't grapple with the ice that develops around December 1, and stays until about April 1.

The winter of 1871 had been harsh, and the giant ice fields in the northern ends of the lakes lingered longer than usual, causing trouble for the boats that were loaded and waiting to get underway. Shipping was delayed on Lake Superior and at the Sault Ste. Marie locks until sometime in May. Boats that plied the lower lakes found that enough ice was in place to cause trouble for them as well.

The small steamer *John Stewart,* under command of Captain John Stewart, was one of the eager vessels. The *Stewart* left Bay City, Michigan, during the third week in March with a cargo bound for Sebewaing, on Lake Huron's Saginaw Bay. The boat got stuck in the ice about a mile and one-half short of its destination.

Stewart and his crew spent five days there, hoping that the ice would melt away and free the vessel before supplies of food and fuel ran out. It didn't happen. On the fifth day, the food ran out. The men waited another two days and still the ship remained caught in the ice. They said the *Stewart* could go neither forward nor back. Things were getting desperate.

The people in Sebewaing had been watching the stranded vessel and had a notion that the crew might be getting hungry. On the eighth day, a team of volunteers managed to get out on the ice, possibly with the help of a small boat, and bring food. The team was warmly received. Captain Stewart sent a message ashore to have a tug come from Bay City and pull his boat free.

The *Stewart* was lucky and survived the incident. The ship remained on the lakes two more seasons before it was destroyed by fire in November, 1872.

The steamer *Marine City* also got lucky when it stranded in Lake Huron ice, although her Detroit owners had a few anxious days. The steamer, under the command of Capt. John Robertson, sailed from Detroit for Cheboygan late in March, only to be locked in ice at Cheboygan.

The *Manitawauba Chronicle,* published in Cheboygan, noted that the *Marine City* arrived in a blinding snow storm, then became blocked in ice a few feet away from the docks. The paper said Robertson and the ship's crew spent about a week in the community, waiting for the wind to shift and the ice to blow back out. The new telegraph cables, under construction all along the coast that year, were not connected at Cheboygan so Robertson couldn't get word back to Detroit that things were all right.

Thus it was on March 31, at about the time the wind shifted to the west and the ice began to blow out of the harbor, that the steamer *Lake Breeze* arrived from Bay City with a delegation of company men on a search and rescue mission. They were concerned that the steamer was either lost or aground someplace along the shore.

It was not the *Marine City's* time. The one hundred and ninety-two-foot long wood hulled steamer remained in service on the lakes for another nine years as a freight and passenger hauler. It burned off Sturgeon Point in 1880.

Making Way for Monsters

The ice was one problem, but for shippers wanting to get their vessels through the Sault Ste. Marie locks and into Lake Superior there was another man-made dilemma. A two and a half million dollar government improvement project had been going on at the locks and channel for about a year which was creating a traffic jam.

The work, which included the deepening and widening of the rock lined channel through which ships reached the locks from Lake Superior, required damming off the water and then using dynamite and sheer manpower to cut the channel to the desired new size. Much of this work was done during the winter, when ships were not passing. A small army of men moved the stone while an elaborate steam powered pumping system kept the channel free of seeping water from Lake Superior and the St. Marys River. The entire project, which took over ten years to complete, also included rebuilding the locks to allow ships with sixteen feet of draft, up to five hundred and ten feet in length, and up to fifteen hundred tons of cargo to pass.

The fact that such locks were on the drawing boards was a sign that planners with vision were around Washington those days. The successful lobbying by shipping companies and other commercial interests probably had a lot to do with it. Before 1871, it would have been impractical to build very large boats for commercial hauling between Lakes Superior and Huron. The size of vessels had been controlled by the two original locks at Sault Ste. Marie, completed in 1855, which measured three hundred and fifty feet in length, and offered a draught of only twelve feet. While there weren't many ships sailing the lakes that were three hundred and fifty feet long in 1871, it was the twelve-foot draught that created the limits of size for vessels locking their way between the lakes.

The bark *Richard Winslow*, first of a new larger class of sailing vessels built to take advantage of the improved locks, demonstrated the problem dramatically that spring when it tried to lock through with a heavy cargo of railroad iron from Cleveland to Duluth. The work of deepening and widening had been started, but it was not finished. A story in the *Houghton Mining Journal* said the *Winslow* had to unload part of its cargo to get through the channel. "She lightened up to (a draught of) eleven feet, two inches and then dragged her bottom the whole length of the channel, and finally reached Duluth in a leaky condition," the story said. The *Winslow's* problem was intensified by a drop in normal lake water levels. A severe drought that prevailed in the midwest throughout 1871 made this problem even worse in later months. The *Winslow* later sailed to Houghton for a cargo of iron ore, but then sank at the dock in twelve feet of water on June 9. The boat was raised and repaired.

The *Winslow* had a capacity for eight hundred and eighty-five tons, while the schooner *D. P. Rhodes,* built that year in the Jones Shipyard at Detroit, measured nine hundred and thirty-three tons and was believed for a while to be the largest freight hauler on the lakes. Another new "giant" was the eight hundred and forty-three-ton schooner *James Couch,* launched at Port Huron, which that year carried a record cargo of sixty thousand bushels of corn. The largest cargo before that was carried by the *W. T. Graves,* which measured fifty-four thousand bushels on a single trip. While the *Graves* was still considered among the bigger boats in 1871, its cargo capacity was reduced because the boat had been converted from a schooner into a steam barge. A large part of the ship housed engines and fuel bunkers.

It seems strange to consider that these new "monster" ships coming down the ways in 1871 were dwarfs in comparison to modern thousand-foot long ore carriers. As noted in an earlier story, the *Couch,* hailed as a super ship in its day, measured only two hundred and ten feet in length.

Striking Sailors

At Chicago, Ill.
Saturday, April 1

The long winter wait was nearly over. A large fleet of ships lay anchored at Chicago, their holds laden with grain from the 1870 harvest, all awaiting the ice blockade at the Straits of Mackinaw to melt away so the busy shipping season could get underway. Also gathering at Chicago were the hundreds of sailors and dock workers who would soon be serving these boats. They spent their idle time playing cards, drinking at the local taverns, and talking.

The word got around that sailors might be in a good position to hold out their services for higher pay. Rumors flew that some of the sailors were striking for higher wages. Organizers of the strike said they were tired of risking their lives and living in dangerous, uncomfortable conditions for a mere dollar and fifty-cents a day. The pay they received was not out of line with the money earned by laborers in 1871. The sailors just wanted more.

When some ship owners gave in and offered a dollar and seventy-five cents, the sailors said they were holding out for three and a quarter. The stalemate was still causing problems when word came that the straits were clear. The boats were firing up to leave port. Their owners were anxious to get the grain delivered and seasonal profits coming in. The grain merchants were biting at the stumps of their cigars. The pressure was on.

A few vessels got underway, manned by sailors who broke down and accepted the offered wage of a dollar and seventy-five cents a day. Other boats remained anchored in the harbor for lack of crews. They included the barks *Mary Perew, J. G. Masten* and *C. J. Wells,* and the schooners *Donaldson, Pathfinder* and *Champion.*

Crazy Days Waiting to Ship Out

At Buffalo, N.Y.
Monday, April 3

Capt. Charles Payment and Capt. Thomas Hubert were mutual acquaintances. They both lived in Detroit and apparently worked for the same shipping line. When their boats were both caught by early winter storms at Buffalo in November, 1870, they were unexpectedly thrust into an uncomfortable situation.

Payment, skipper of the bark *H. C. Winslow,* either had his wife aboard ship on his last trip, or else he brought her to Buffalo by train to spend the winter with him in a rented house near the waterfront. It was a place where he could keep an eye on the *Winslow.* Captain Hubert, master of the schooner *Columbian,* was invited to move in with the Payments. He shared the rent and probably got his meals thrown in with the deal.

The arrangement might have gone well, but it turned out that Hubert and Payment had different life styles and personalities. Their apparent inability to handle those differences while living under the same roof led to serious trouble.

Payment appeared to be a devoted husband who believed in staying at home and abstaining from the evils of alcoholism, prostitution and gambling, all of which tempted sailors along the wharves in 1871. Hubert, on the other hand, was alone that long winter. If he had a wife, she was not with him. He fell prey to the vices of the town, and that bothered Payment.

Things festered until one day, late in March, the two men had a serious argument. Some said Payment threatened to report Hubert's activities to the shipping line in Detroit and possibly get him fired. Hubert brooded over the threat for several days. Then, according to local police reports and newspaper accounts, he entered Payment's bedroom at about 2:00 AM on the morning of April 3, and asked the captain to come outside to have a word. Payment obliged, and since it was still early spring on Lake Erie, probably took a moment to get dressed.

Once he emerged from the house, Hubert drew a revolver and pointed it at Payment's head. He said he had decided to kill Payment. Hubert didn't want to do the murder there in front of the house. He ordered Payment to walk a few blocks to the lake, apparently planning to dispose of the body in the water once the deed was done.

Payment stumbled along that morning with his hands held high in the air and with Hubert's firearm pointing directly at his head. No longer groggy from sleep, his mind was racing. He frantically tried to think of a way out of this dilemma. As the two men stepped between two cottages, Payment make a break for freedom. He reasoned that he had nothing to lose, and made a dash for the nearby beach.

He was very lucky. Hubert pulled the trigger the moment Payment made his move, but the gun failed to fire on the first shot. Hubert fired off five other rounds, but all of the bullets missed. Payment jumped over a sea wall and dove into the water, where he made his escape.

Police were notified. They had Hubert arrested and in jail by 7:30 AM.

Deadly Collision

Off Chicago Harbor
Lake Michigan
Friday, April 7

The spring shipping season was finally underway and the tug *S. V. R. Watson,* under command of Captain Frank Green was busy. The *Watson* was hired by the schooner *S. G. Simmons* for a customary tow out of the harbor and into Lake Michigan. The *Simmons* was departing on a trip north to Kenosha, Wisconsin.

All was going well. Then at noon, when the two vessels got just outside the south pier and the *Watson* was about to cast off the tow line, something went wrong and the *Watson* was overrun by the *Simmons.* The tug capsized, and Captain Green plus three other men were drowned.

There were two stories. The *Detroit Daily Post* said the crew of the *Simmons* hoisted sail too early, and stiff winds caused the schooner to overrun the tug before the crew could get the tow line disconnected. That account was repeated in the official report to the Board of Supervising Inspectors of Steam Vessels the following year.

The other story, published in newspapers along the Lake Michigan coast, said the tug stalled and was overrun by the *Simmons*. The stalled engine story may have been true. It would explain why an experienced tugboat crew was lax in dropping a tow line at about the time the vessel under tow was raising sail. The fact that Captain Green and Louis B. Johnson, the tug's owner, left the pilot house to go below at that moment also suggests that there was some kind of trouble in the engine room requiring their attention.

The schooner hit the *Watson* broadside, causing the smaller vessel to tip violently on its beam ends, take on water and sink. Green, Johnson, and crew members John Garrity and Patrick Waters were trapped below deck. Two other unnamed sailors survived.

The *Watson* was raised and returned to service.

Port Huron Traffic Jam

On the St. Clair River
Port Huron, Mich.
Saturday, April 8

Sooner or later, all ships on the Great Lakes pass through the St. Clair River. That narrow body of fast flowing water, connecting Lake Huron with Lake St. Clair, the Detroit River and Lake Erie beyond, may be one of the busiest shipping channels in the world. It is part of the modern St. Lawrence Seaway. It always was the key link for vessels carrying goods and passengers between Chicago and Buffalo, or ore and grain from Duluth to ports along Lake Erie.

It should not be surprising, then, to know that accidents have been common on the St. Clair River. The rotted hulls of many old wrecks still can be found on the river bottom.

Sometimes the collisions among vessels at Port Huron were so involved it is hard now to tell the stories with a straight face. Consider the incident that happened on April 8, 1871.

It started when the skipper of the schooner *A. Mosher* saw that he had a favorable wind and decided to save the price of a tow by tugboat. The *Mosher* made the trip up the river, from the St. Clair Flats to Port Huron, under sail. All went well until the *Mosher* passed Port Huron on the final leg of the trip. The boat got too close to the river bank, struck some old dock timbers and went out of control. The *Mosher* was driven out into the busy river, all canvass set and the wind pushing it headlong into certain disaster. The runaway boat collided with the downbound three masted schooner *H. C. Post*. The crash carried away the *Post's* main and foremasts and all of the forward rigging and sails.

The two captains dropped anchor in mid-stream, at about the point where the Black River joins the St. Clair River, and argued over compensation for damages. Then the *Mosher,* which still had its sails intact, continued on its way. The captain of the *Post* made an unwise decision when he left his ship anchored at that spot, in the middle of two busy rivers and went ashore to arrange for repairs.

While he was gone, the schooner *Jesse Anderson* sailed smartly out of the Black River and drove its bow right into the side of the *Post*. The collision smashed six of the *Post's* stanchions, and finished wrecking the ropes, crosstrees, pulleys and sails on the stern mast.

The accident threw the *Anderson* out of control and it went aground on the river bank. The tug *George H. Parker* came to the *Anderson's* rescue and also went aground in the mud bank, right alongside the *Anderson*. The two vessels remained stuck there for several hours before the *Parker* worked its way off and pulled the *Anderson* free.

Rammed Off Port Hope

On Lake Huron
At Port Hope, Mich.
Saturday, April 8

A northeast gale on Lake Huron was cooking up some serious trouble for the tugboat *Satellite*. The tug, believed to have been commanded that spring by Capt. William Moore, met the bark *James C. King* and attempted to take it under tow at about 8:00 PM.

The *King* was under canvas and running before a stiff wind. When the *Satellite* steamed across the bow of the surging bark the two boats came in collision. The *King* drove its bow deep into the side of the tug, causing the *Satellite* to keel hard over for a few anxious moments. When the bows of the bark slid away, the tug righted itself again.

The crash knocked the *Satellite's* first mate, Chester Stewart, of Harsons Island, Michigan, overboard and he was drowned.

The *King* still had canvas set and the bark was blown off into the night, not to be seen again. The *Satellite* was left wallowing in the storm with a hole in its side, the fires out, and taking on water.

Crew members bailed for their lives that night until the tug *Quayle* noticed a lantern of distress and steamed out of Port Hope harbor to take her in tow. The *Quayle* arrived just in time. The stricken tug sank in fourteen feet of water just outside the harbor but the crew was saved.

The vessel was later raised.

The steam barge *Bay City* got caught up in a lumber yard fire on the Saginaw River.

Fire on the Bay City

On the Saginaw River
Near Bay City, Mich.
Sunday, April 9

The propeller barge *Bay City* was a victim of some-body else's fire. The boat, under the command that spring of a Captain Clark, had completed one trip, hauling lumber from the Rust and Company mill on the Saginaw River to Tonawanda, and was back in port, nearly loaded with two hundred and seventy thousand feet of new cargo for a second trip.

The *Bay City* was tied up at the mill dock, near Bay City, apparently waiting out the gale that was sweeping the lakes that weekend, when fire broke out in a nearby lumber pile at about 11:00 AM. There quickly developed a spectacular conflagration that brought three fire departments to the scene. Before they could become spectators, the crew of the *Bay City* first needed to save their ship from the advancing flames. The engineer didn't have steam up. The lines were cast off and the vessel was allowed to drift off down the river until a tug towed it to a dock farther down stream.

Once they believed the ship was safe, the crew turned its attention to events on shore as large piles of lumber, company supplies from a winter of work in the forests along the Saginaw River, went up in smoke. At about 2:00 PM, someone noticed smoke billowing out of the steamer's hold. A spark from the lumber fire apparently had fallen through an open hatch. The blaze had smoldered for an hour or two before it got a good start, deep in the cargo of wood.

The crew manned the ship's hand-operated pumps, but the water they were pouring on the fire seemed to be doing little good. Harbor tugs came alongside and began pumping streams of water from their steam powered pumps. The persistent fire was not to be conquered. Later, after four tugs joined the battle and a steam-powered fire engine was brought alongside on a lighter, and they still couldn't get the fire out, the decision was made to scuttle the ship. The sinking was messy, but it saved the steamer and much of its cargo.

The *Bay City*, owned by businessmen from Marine City, Michigan, was raised a few days later and repaired. The damage was reported at four thousand dollars, which was a lot in 1871. The ship plied the lakes another twenty years before burning a second time to a total loss at Detroit.

The *Bay City* was built in 1867 at Marine City. It was a wooden hulled propeller, measuring one hundred and fifty-two feet in length. Arches, used to strengthen the hulls of wooden ships of that period, were added in March, 1871, only weeks before the first fire.

Adrift on Lake Michigan

Somewhere in Mid-lake
Wednesday, April 19

The brigantine *St. Joseph* left Ludington, Michigan on Monday morning, extra heavily laden with lumber and bound for Chicago. In their eagerness to insure a profit on each trip, lake captains sometimes gambled by overloading their boats. The *St. Joseph* was among them. Lumber was not only crammed in the holds, but a second cargo was stacked as high as it could go on the open decks without interfering with the swing of the sail booms. A gale developed and the top-heavy boat began to roll. The cables holding down the deck load couldn't take the pressure and they started to break.

When the cargo started going by the boards, the shifting cargo caused the boat to list and take on water. By the time the deck load was gone, the ship was in a state the sailors called "being waterlogged." That meant that for all practical purposes, the ship was sunk. Unless the ballast was extra heavy, wooden ships filled with wooden cargo didn't actually sink. They became mostly submerged.

A waterlogged sailing ship with a deck load sometimes capsized. Being waterlogged was an especially dangerous condition for the sailors because it meant they were going to spend some time in the water, on a ship that was partly sunk, out of control, and possibly tipped over. Their options were to abandon ship in an open boat, or hang on and wait for help.

The *St. Joseph* remained upright, but the cabins were flooded and there was no place for the sailors to stay warm and dry. From Monday night until Wednesday morning, the crew chose to remain with the ship. The only food was a ham that someone rescued from the galley. It was a long and dismal ordeal. The rough weather continued and the men were constantly soaked from waves that repeatedly crashed over them.

The propeller *St. Lewis* found them on Wednesday morning about thirty-five miles southwest of Pentwater and took them into that port. The tug *Aldrich* later found the brig, still partially sunk, and towed it in.

Insuring Safety on Steamships

Fires were common on the early steamboats. The boats also had a tendency to spring leaks and sink, explode their boilers, and run aground during storms or on foggy days. They collided with one another, or broke down in the middle of the lake and floated until a passing boat found them or they drifted ashore. The statistics indicated that steamboats were not safe. Yet there were so many of them coming and going on the lakes in the 1870s, and the roads and railroad lines were so primitive across the Michigan, Ohio and Wisconsin, people traveled by boat much as they do by automobile today. Anyone unfortunate enough to be aboard a ship that burned or sank was bound to endure extreme hardship and even death. It was a fact of life, not only on the Great Lakes, but also on the oceans.

The government began passing laws to set safety standards for steamboats that carried passengers almost as soon as these ships began service. Congress passed the first of many acts in 1838, only thirty-one years after Robert Fulton's famous steamboat *Clermont* made its historic voyage. The Steamboat Act of 1852 established the Steamboat Inspection Service. That act created nine inspection districts, each with a supervising inspector who had responsibility over local hull and boiler inspectors.

Rivalries developed among the district supervisors, so Congress moved on Feb. 28, 1871, to create the position of Supervising Inspector General in charge of district supervisors. That person was appointed by the President and approved by the Senate. He served under the Department of Treasury.

The Act of 1871 also drafted tougher steamboat safety laws and for the first time, it extended the same rights and protection previously afforded only to passengers, to the officers and crew members aboard steamboats. While important, the laws for safety aboard the ships were relatively simple compared to standards set by contemporary law, but they made common sense in their day.

For example, U. S. Inspectors were asking vessels to carry enough life preservers for everybody to have one in case of trouble. Passenger boats also were required to carry five watchmen to look out for fire. Two watchmen were to be stationed on the main deck, two in the cabins and one on the hurricane deck.

The laws required the owners of steamboats in passenger service to employ a competent number of experienced engineers to operate their steam engines, to have hulls inspected annually and the boilers inspected every six months.

Lifeboats, fire pumps and hose and signal lights were required on all vessels. The owner had to obtain a license showing that he met the requirements before he could carry passengers. Other laws required steamboats to carry emergency steering apparatus, and set limits for passengers.

There was one other law that helped people on shore track the boats as they moved through the lakes. It required each ship to have its name clearly showing in large, easy to read letters on both sides of the hull. Because there was no way for ships to communicate with their owners in 1871, the only way for anyone to know their whereabouts was for ships and lighthouse keepers to record each vessel passed. People on shore also kept records at key places like Detroit, Port Huron, or Sault Ste. Marie. Names that were easy to read became an important link between the ship's crews and the outside world.

Break in the Wall

On the Erie Canal
Fairport, N. Y.
Friday, April 28

It was about 11:00 PM and Captain Terrill and his steersman were taking turns walking the horses along the bank of the canal as they pulled the empty scow *Barney Bird* westward on a trip to Buffalo. As they approached the Ox Bow, a twisting branch of the canal where an artificial wall was built to separate a small lake and open meadow, the wall collapsed. Terrill later described the noise as sounding something like a giant steam engine.

The *Barney Bird* was about eight hundred feet away from the break. Terrill and his helper tried to snub the craft, but the force of the fast moving water was too great. The tow line parted and the scow was swept off through the opening into the dark night, carrying Terrill, his wife and child, the steersman plus a team of horses on a wild ride into no-man's land.

Good fortune was with the family that night. The vessel floated upright across a field and came to a stop undamaged against an elm tree about a half mile from where it passed through the break. Nobody was hurt. Everybody spent a strange night aboard the ship, waiting for morning to come so they could find out exactly what had happened to them and assess the damage.

Other animals and buildings in the way of the rushing water didn't fare as well. At least one cow was killed, a barn destroyed, and a few trees were uprooted. One report said debris was found hanging from tree limbs fifteen feet in the air after the water went down.

Days past before the barge was refloated, and about two weeks went by before the canal was repaired. To get the job done, a work force of eight hundred men, plus one hundred and seventy teams of horses were put on the job both night and day until the canal was reopened.

A nasty labor strike stopped the work for a day on May 4. The Army Reserves were summoned to the scene to restore order and two men, named Smith and Williams, were arrested on charges of starting a riot, resisting arrest and assaulting police officers. The troops stood by after that until the job was finished. The canal was an important artery carrying goods from Great Lakes ports to the Atlantic coast. Its shut-down forced vessels to take the long route across Lake Ontario and down the St. Lawrence River.

Buffalo, where the Erie Canal began, was soon feeling the pinch. The *Buffalo Commercial Advertiser* reported a twenty percent drop in business at the harbor within a few days. Everybody was glad when the canal was reopened on about May 12.

Early dock scene when the *Forester* was a steamer. The boat was a stripped-down lumber barge when it grounded on Lake Erie in 1871.

Wreck of the *Forester*

On Lake Erie
Wednesday, May 3

The *Forester* was one of three ancient lumber barges under tow behind the steam barge *D. F. Rose,* plying between Saginaw and Toledo. It nearly ended its career when the four vessels got caught in a gale at the western end of Lake Erie on May 3.

The storm grew in intensity and the tow line parted, forcing the crews of the *Forester* and barges *Mary Stockton* and *United* to hoist sail and continue along on their own. Both the *Stockton* and *United* scampered before the northeaster to Toledo where they ducked into the Maumee River. The storm was severe enough that they lost their deck loads of lumber.

The *Forester* went aground and took a beating before the storm ended. The crew escaped unharmed. The barge was salvaged that year and put back in service, still hauling lumber. It's time on the lakes was nearly over, however. The *For-*

ester sank in another storm in September, 1872, also on Lake Erie. The ship was originally built in 1854 as a wooden passenger steamer by Newport, Michigan ship builder J. Bushnell for shipping giant E. B. Ward. It plied regularly between Detroit and Port Huron before being converted as a barge. The boat measured one hundred and ninety-six feet in length.

Eight Lost Soldiers

On Lake Ontario
Fort Niagara, N. Y.
Thursday, May 4

The same storm that wrecked the *Forester* was creating havoc at Fort Niagara, on the western end of Lake Ontario. Lt. J. Campbell Morrison, acting commanding officer for the day, noticed that a small government-owned row boat had broken loose from it's moorings on the Niagara River and drifted out into the lake.

Morrison and Lt. George Ashbury organized a party of six other volunteer soldiers and took them out in a second boat to recover the wayward craft. The other volunteers were Cpl. George T. Hobbs, and privates George Dowle, Francis Pierce, George F. Hadley, Patrick Mooney and Thomas Sharkey. They left the fort at 11:00 AM in a thirty-foot boat and began rowing for the missing craft, by then located about three miles to the west and not far off shore. When they reached their target two hours later, they were drifted seven miles west of the fort and about a quarter of a mile off shore, clearly in sight of a small group of people who were gathered to watch from shore. Their craft was being battered about by high wind and waves.

Witnesses said the men turned their boat toward shore and someone, believed to have been Morrison, stood up in the stern as if to sight a landing place. A wave jostled the boat at that same moment and Morrison fell overboard. The others apparently moved over in a collective effort to rescue Morrison and capsized the boat. It all happened within seconds.

The boat floated keel up and only five people could be seen clinging to it. The soldiers were no match for the stinging cold waters of Lake Ontario. Overheated from hours of hard rowing, they died quickly. One-by-one the unfortunate men slipped off into the water as the cold claimed them.

George Dowle, one of the strongest men at the fort, was still clinging to the overturned boat when it drifted about two hundred feet from shore. Then he also fell away and was seen no more. Their bodies and both boats washed ashore later.

Swept Over Niagara Falls

Niagara Falls, N. Y.
Thursday, May 18

A writer for the *Buffalo Courier* theorized that the three men may have been fugitives, attempting to flee to Canada. Nobody was ever sure about their names. They were believed to be in their mid-20s. One account said James Murphy was among them. Still another story said that the other two may have been George Fowle and a companion known as Coddington, who left Rochester, New York a few weeks earlier with plans to travel west.

The three made a fatal mistake when they tried to cross the Niagara River in an open boat, a short distance above the mighty Horseshoe Falls.

They had appeared at Walker's Boat House at about 4:15 PM and asked to rent a boat for a trip to a little nearby island. They said they wanted to swim there and then return. The Walkers were reluctant to rent the boat because they knew how dangerous the river was, and also saw that these men were strangers to the area. The three said they understood the danger and promised to keep near shore and within safety limits of the island.

The Walkers watched the men cross to the island, and then they were horrified when the boys didn't stop as promised, but began rowing their way out into the fast-moving river current. It appeared as if they were trying to cross over into Canada. The boat got caught in the rapids and capsized, dumping all three men in the water. The word of the pending disaster spread like wildfire along the river.

As the three floated past one small island, local natives risked their lives wading out in the fast current and trying to grab them as they passed. One of the men came within five feet of safety, but then floated by, heading for certain destruction. People said two of the men appeared to have drowned by the time their bodies passed over the falls.

Last Days of the *B. B. Jones*

At Port Huron, Mich.
Thursday, May 25

Even though an important pump that fed water to the boiler was malfunctioning, Capt. Samuel H. Burnham decided against shutting down for a day and give chief engineer Thomas Blanchard time to fix it. The decision may have led to the explosion that wrecked his ship, the tug *B. B. Jones,* and killed eight of the twelve men who served it.

The chance of earning some good salvage money that week at Cove Island probably influenced Burnham. Business was competitive and brisk in the spring of 1871. After just completing some expensive repairs and renovating, the tug's owners, Trowbridge and Wilcox, probably let Burnham know they were in no mood to let a bad pump make them pass up any opportunity to generate a cash return on their investment. The tempting carrot was the lumber bark *City of Buffalo,* which had gone aground on Cove Island. Burnham took the job and preparations were made to leave immediately.

The *City of Buffalo* holed itself on a reef near the island on May 18. The crew spent one day shifting the cargo of lumber and then working the vessel free, only to find that the boat was leaking so badly they had to turn back to the island and let it sink in shallow water. Cove Island is a rocky obstacle located one hundred and fifty miles north of Port Huron in the main channel separating Lake Huron from Georgian Bay. Many boats lie in ruins there after hitting the dangerous reefs and sinking among the rocks.

The *B. B. Jones* steamed out of Port Huron harbor late on the afternoon of Saturday, May 20, with a full load of coal, canvass, hawsers and a portable steam pump aboard.

Blanchard, in an effort to make sure his hard working boiler was getting the water it needed to make steam, decided sometime during the trip to disconnect the faulty pump and rig a portable pump to replace it. The device seemed to work.

Salvaging the *City of Buffalo* was a tricky job, but the crew of the *Jones* was used to the work. A steam pump was put on the bark's deck and Burnham may also have chained canvas around the hull to slow the volume of water coming through the hole. Hawsers then were attached. After most of the water was pumped out of the hull, the *Jones* began using its powerful engines to pull the wreck away from the island and back into the open waters of Lake Huron.

The *Jones* steamed back to Port Huron the following Wednesday, May 24, with the *City of Buffalo* in tow. The ship's owners then ordered the *Jones* to continue on to Detroit and deliver the damaged vessel there for unloading and repair. From Detroit, the *Jones* picked up a string of five barges and schooners that needed a tow back up the river to Lake Huron. The tug returned to Port Huron on Thursday morning, docking at the Port Huron and Lake Michigan Railroad dock, where two more ships, the schooner *Aidebaran* and the scow *Preble* were waiting for a tow back down the river.

Burnham, anxious to keep his tug working while the work was available, decided once again to ignore the faulty pump and try to get by as long as possible with things the way they were. He did not know that time was running out. As the ship lay at the dock, its boilers still hot and waiting to depart for still another trip down the St. Clair River, the cook, J. W. Jones, gave the call to dinner. The crew filed into the mess for what they thought was going to be a noon meal. Instead, the sailors were stepping into a death trap.

The force of the hot blast ripped through a fire wall and passed directly through the mess, killing seven sailors instantly. Burnham and four other men, Charles Marsh, Patrick Reed, David Martin and Jones were still alive after the blast, but Jones died a day or two later from burns. Also killed were Mate Andrew Rathbun, Algonac; First Engineer Blanchard, Detroit; Second Engineer Hugh Campbell, Detroit; wheelsmen Patrick McGuire, Malden, and Adeibert Preston, Detroit; fireman Charles Miller, Detroit, and a seventh man, not identified.

Burnham said he was sitting at the table in his cabin, eating his dinner one moment, and next found himself struggling in the river. He was seriously injured but alive. It was theorized that the blast lifted him up with the deck. The force of the explosion cut the heavy deck beams beneath his feet like pipe stems. His chair was torn to pieces. The *Jones* was destroyed and what was left of the tug sank immediately alongside the dock.

Witnesses said the blast shattered the ship into a million pieces, hurling fragments of wood, iron and flesh hundreds of feet in every direction. Sailors on the *Aidebaran* saw what happened and began lowering a lifeboat, expecting to use it to pick up survivors. Before it hit the water, however, a huge chunk of the *Jones'* boiler fell from the sky and destroyed the boat, missing the sailors and the stern of the schooner by inches. Another large piece of the boiler demolished a building several hundred feet away. A large piece of flying iron struck a home in the western part of Port Huron, about a quarter of a mile away. Miraculously, nobody else in the area was hurt. All of the survivors were pulled from the river. They had literally been thrown from the ship by the blast. Only one body was removed from the water in one piece. Divers later began the gruesome task of removing pieces of bone and flesh from what was left of the sunken wreck.

A report to the Board of Supervising Inspectors of Steam Vessels noted that the boiler on the *Jones* was inspected on April 20, just 24 days before it exploded. The official investigation revealed that return water tubes were collapsed, indicating that the explosion was caused by low water in the boiler. Blanchard's make-shift pump had failed.

The *Jones* was a wood hulled vessel, built by B. B. Jones at Milwaukee in 1864.

Steam barge *R. J. Hackett* was one of many boats hung up in the shallow water at the St. Clair River Flats in 1871.

Saga of the *R. J. Hackett*

On the St. Clair River Flats
Near Marine City, Mich.
Saturday, May 27

The steam barge *R. J. Hackett* was traveling empty, with the bark *Homer* in tow, on its way up the lakes to Escanaba, Michigan, when it hit bottom and jerked to a stop in the notorious St. Clair Flats.

Grounding at the flats was a common problem faced by ship's captains and owners in 1871. The St. Clair Flats is a muddy, shallow delta where the St. Clair River empties into Lake St. Clair, which in turn is a shallow basin of water that separates the St. Clair and Detroit Rivers.

The United States government opened a channel through the flats in 1858 that allowed vessels with a draft of less than eleven feet to pass, but as bigger vessels were built, the channel was no longer adequate. A new dredging operation was being completed there in 1871. Plans were to open a second channel thirteen feet deep. The job wasn't finished and an unusually dry period caused lake levels to drop which created more of an obstacle.

Thus it was on May 27 that the *Hackett,* commanded by a Captain Trotter, and a second steamer, the *Dean Richmond,* Capt. James Pratt, both found themselves stuck in the mud on the same day. The two boats may have been attempting to pass each other in the same narrow channel.

A battery of tugs and other vessels was called upon. Getting ships unstuck was a full-time job that season. No sooner did a vessel get hung-up, then a parade of waiting ships began backing up on both the St. Clair River and in Lake St. Clair, waiting for the channel to be re-opened. Some reports told of as many as forty to fifty vessels anchored, waiting to pass.

This time the problem was serious. The *Richmond* was pulled free on Sunday afternoon, the day after it went aground, but the *Hackett* didn't get off until June 5, nine days later. The problem was that the *Hackett* was traveling without cargo. When a ship is loaded, it rides lower in the water. The job of getting a laden vessel worked free again usually involves removal of cargo. In the *Hackett's* case, there was nothing except the boat's own fuel bunkers of coal to take off, and that was done. It was said that the tugs pulled so hard that the *Hackett's* stern posts gave way. The Coast Wrecking Company was called. Dredges dug a new trench under the ship. Giant pontoons were attached to both sides of the hull and inflated. Once given the extra buoyancy, the stranded steamer was finally pulled free.

Bad luck followed the *Hackett* on that trip. As it steamed on up Lake Huron on the night of June 8, the boat got in pea-soup fog and then grounded at Thunder Bay Island. This time the tugs *Prindiville* and *Satellite* worked for several days before pulling her free again on June 12.

The *Hackett* was not an easy vessel to pull out of the mud. It measured two hundred and eight feet long and thirty-two feet, five inches at the beam. This ship held the honor of being the first ship of its kind designed specifically to carry iron ore and a forerunner of the modern ore carrier.

Lightning

On Lake Huron
Friday, June 2

Lightning bolts are a natural menace to ships at sea. Any vessel stands tall above the water and becomes a target during an electric storm.

The barge *Banner,* laden with six hundred and thirty-two tons of iron ore, was under tow across Lake Huron behind the steamer *Concord* when a summer storm developed. Lightning struck the *Banner's* fore-topmast, then jumped to the foremast, struck the deck, and then followed the ship's chains to the water. The bold knocked the mate and ship's cook off their feet, but neither man was seriously hurt. The mast was shattered and had to be replaced.

Wreck of the Maitland

At the Straits of Mackinaw
Sunday, June 11

The bark *Maitland,* under command of a Captain Brown, was scudding before a fresh night breeze, making its way through the Straits of Mackinaw with a full load of corn from Chicago, when disaster struck. Out of the dark came the schooner *Golden Harvest,* under command of Capt. Francis B. Higgie. Without warning the two vessels collided almost head-on. The crash was so violent, both ships were demasted. Sails, masts, ropes and tackle toppled on the sailors below.

The *Golden Harvest's* bow hit the *Maitland* just forward the anchor, opening up the bark's hull. Already seriously damaged and sinking, the *Maitland* continued along, out of control, and slammed into the side of the nearby three-masted schooner *C. Mears,* with Captain Grant at the helm, carrying away some of the sails and rigging on the *Mears.* As the *Maitland* began settling, the crew successfully launched a lifeboat and escaped.

The *Golden Harvest* remained afloat, but the vessel was in a serious condition. The schooner's bow was crushed, it was leaking badly, and without sails, it was drifting before the wind. To make matters worse, three crew members aboard the *Golden Harvest* were seriously hurt. The second mate, said to have been a brother to Captain Higgie, was apparently hit on the head by a falling spar. He was suffering from a skull fracture and not expected to live. A forward lookout was said to have suffered a broken leg, and the wheelsman fractured a rib when he was thrown into the wheel.

39

The *Maitland* went down about five miles east of Wangoshance light in one hundred and sixty-seven fathoms. The accident happened at about ten o'clock. The bark had sailed the lakes for twenty years before it was lost.

Rescue Aboard the *William A. Moore*

On Saginaw Bay
Lake Huron
Monday, June 19

Captain W. H. O'Neill, skipper of the tug *William A. Moore,* knew his wife and son, Walter, were going to drown if he didn't get them out of the cabin of his sinking ship. The tug, engaged in hauling log rafts from the Saginaw River to Detroit, tipped to its side on Saginaw Bay from the weight of fuel piled too high on the open decks. O'Neill saw that the boat was going to the bottom.

When the tug started to topple to port, he said he signaled the engineer to stop the engines, then ran toward the cabin to rescue his family. An unidentified watchman helped O'Neill force open the door and pull the woman and child up through it, even as the water was filling the room. It was a desperate moment, but everybody got out of the boat safely before it settled in thirty-nine feet of water.

The accident happened at about 6:30 PM, about two hours after the *Moore* left Bay City. The tug was steaming north to pick up a raft of pine logs at Point au Gres when it capsized and settled by the stern about four miles off the mouth of the Rifle River. An air pocked remained trapped in the bow, causing that part of the tug to float for a while after the stern touched the bottom of the lake.

The O'Neills and the ship's crew, fourteen people in all, gathered around the smoke stack, hoisted signals of distress, and then clung to the partly submerged wreck for two hours before help arrived. The life boat couldn't be launched because it was attached at the sunken stern. One man dove three times in an attempt to cut the boat loose from the davits, but he was not successful.

The lake was calm when the accident first happened, but a breeze from the east northeast developed and a sea began to rise. O'Neill worried that the bow portion of the tug would also settle. The shipwreck victims were disappointed when the tug *Anna Moiles* steamed by with a log raft in tow and didn't stop. The *Moiles'* captain, a man named Mitchell, said he couldn't get free of his tow, but that he signaled to Captain Eastman, on the nearby tug *Coleman,* which made the rescue.

The *Moore* was raised and towed to Bay City around the end of June. Its stack, pilot house and cabin were gone. The tug was refitted and returned to service.

Lumber Rafting

A common sight on the Great Lakes in 1871 was that of large lumber rafts under tow from the Saginaw Valley and a variety of other ports along Michigan's coast to the processing mills mostly on Lake Erie.

The rafts were invented during the Civil War as a way to beat the high freight rates charged by the shipping companies. When the war created a shortage of boats, fees which originally had been about a dollar and a half for every thousand feet of lumber shipped, jumped to seven and even nine dollars to haul good grade pine to the lower end of Lake Erie.

Rafts were made of several long timbers, usually about forty feet long and about the size of a common telegraph pole, which were chained together. At the sides were secured several upright timbers which were attached at the top again to form a crib. The lumber was usually piled in several floating cribs like this, and the cribs each securely bound to each other to form a floating raft. The raft was pulled by a tug down Lake Huron and through the St. Clair and Detroit Rivers to their destination.

Once the raft was established as a successful way of moving lumber, the tug operators experimented to see how much lumber they could move in a single trip. The newspapers mentioned it each time new records were set. One single crib was sent to Toledo that measured two hundred feet in

The tug *Relief* pulled one of the largest lumber rafts on record down the Detroit River.

length and forty-two feet wide. Some estimated that it contained about fifteen thousand feet of lumber. Tugs challenged each other to set new records for board feet of logs hauled. In July, 1873, the tug *Relief* pulled two rafts at the same time from Wild Foul Bay, Michigan, to Tonawanda, New York, containing twenty-five thousand feet. The rafts included two hundred fifty cribs covering an estimated twelve acres.

It was not uncommon for the lumber men to ride on top of the cribs as they were pulled across the lake. They erected shanties with cooking stoves and makeshift beds in them for the trip. The cribs were usually about fifteen feet high, with about eleven feet submerged in the water.

By 1870 several big companies got organized to use tugs to pull the rafts from Saginaw Bay south into Lake Erie. The companies that used the log rafts included Hoagland of Dayton, Ohio; Mitchell and Rowland Co. of Toledo, Ohio, and W. R. Burt of Saginaw, Mich.

While they proved to be an ingenious way for lumbermen to save costs of getting their product to market, the raft system had its problems. By 1871, the *Detroit Free Press* commented on how the use of rafting to move logs was greatly increased over the year before. The paper also reported several cases where the rafts got loose in bad weather and then blew ashore. Storms tossed thousands of giant logs from these wayward rafts on many shores, smashing docks and docked boats and doing a lot of destruction to private property.

The rafts were large unmarked and unlighted objects afloat on a lake filled with ships of every size and description. When they broke free from the towing ship, and then sometimes broke up, they filled the water with missiles waiting to sink or do great mischief to unwitting ships that hit them. Many a story was told about how logs became tangled in the churning wheels of passing steamboats, smashing the wooden paddles and wrecking the engines that propelled them. Other boats were damaged or even sunk after colliding with floating logs and unlighted log rafts in the lake. Shipping companies complained about the rafts and demanded controls.

The lumber companies were concerned about the problem. Lumber rafters held a special meeting in Detroit on July 6, 1871, to talk about ways of protecting the rafts from collision by ships. It was suggested that lights and horns be installed on them, as if they too were ships. There is no record of lights and horns ever being installed on rafts, however.

There were other concerns. Getting the rafts through the busy St. Clair and Detroit Rivers was no simple task. The large, unwieldy tows sometimes went out of control in the unpredictable current, smashing docks and endangering passing vessels. A few accidents like that kicked off a growing tide of anger and frustration among lakefront property owners. The grumbling was heard in Washington. Thus it was that the use of log rafts was outlawed, and the lumber companies switched to the old proven system of hauling a string of barges behind a single steamboat. They became such a common sight they were called a mother hen and her chicks passing in single file.

Like the raft haulers, tugboat captains tried to outdo one another in the barge strings they were able to tow. In June, 1872, the steamer *Antelope,* under command of Captain R. Vallentine, pulled a tow of eight lumber barges extending over a mile in length down the Detroit River. These boats carried about six million feet of lumber in a single trip.

Lumbering in Michigan was big business in 1871, even after the forests were swept by a major fire. A story in the *Saginaw Courier* in February, 1872, noted that two hundred and fifty men were still employed in the state that winter cutting lumber, lath, shingles and railings for shipment down the lakes, while another four thousand men were working in the mills, producing five million feet of lumber every twelve hours.

The H. W. Sage and Co. of Saginaw was considered one of the largest working lumber mills in the United States in 1871. The company produced over twenty-two million board feet of lumber that year. Other major companies included W. R. Burt and Co., John McGraw and Co. and Sears and Holland, all producing over eighteen million feet each.

The story said nearly one billion, seven million feet of lumber were shipped from Michigan to Chicago, Detroit, Toledo and other ports in 1870 and that the demand was growing. Much of the lumber used in rebuilding Chicago after the great fire of 1871 came from Michigan forests.

SUMMER

Burning of the *Alexander Watson*

On the St. Clair River
Lambton, Ont.
Thursday, June 30

The river steamer *Alexander Watson,* under command of Capt. James R. Inness, was making regular stops along the St. Clair River, when fire broke out in the boiler room.

The ship was just pulling up to the dock at Lambton when the fire was discovered at about 10:00 PM. The crew slammed the vessel up to the dock, then everybody scrambled for safety. It was said the fire had such a start by the time it broke through the deck, it was too late to save the ship. The cargo was wood, which helped fuel the flames.

People gathered to watch the little steamer burn itself into a charred ruin. Eventually the fire burned the mooring ropes and the doomed boat drifted off into the river, a burning spectacle. It drifted aground on Walpole Island where the fire blazed for the rest of the night.

There was a single casualty. The captain's pet terrier was lost.

The *Watson* was built in 1870 at Wallaceburg, Ont. It made regular trips between Wallaceburg, Ontario and Detroit, Michigan.

The *Maine* was a hard luck boat. Several people died when it exploded its boiler in 1871.

Exploding the *Maine*

On Lake Ontario
Off Ogdensburg, N.Y.
Tuesday, July 4

If a "hoodoo" ship ever existed on the lakes, it was the Northern Transportation Company's propeller *Maine*. When the *Maine* exploded its boiler off Ogdensburg on Independence Day, it was the first of five serious disasters that hounded the ship until it burned to destruction at Marine City, Michigan in 1911.

The 1871 explosion was among the more serious of the terrors to sweep the *Maine*. Three sailors and two passengers died in the blast that rocked the ship at about 8:00 PM, just as the steamer was completing passage from Chicago. Fireman Orsebius Kelley, who lived long enough to tell his story, said he had just stoked a fire and went to the porter's room to get a lamp. He said he was returning to the engine room when the boiler blew.

The explosion also killed Engineer M. H. Downer and deck hand Josuha Kelley, the fireman's brother, and a passenger, thirteen-year-old Halbert Butterfield and Butterfield's mother. Mrs. Butterfield was knocked overboard by the blast and not seen again. Orsebius Kelley was badly scalded and he died a day or two later from his injuries. A porter, Allen Cook, also was hurt, but apparently recovered.

The force of the blast passed aft through steerage, but nobody was there at the time. The hull remained intact and the *Maine* did not sink. The ship was repaired.

The steamer sank the following year off Alexandria Bay, New York, burned at Port Huron, Michigan in 1880, burned at Tonawanda, New York in 1898, and burned one final time at Marine City in 1911.

Strange Premonition

The *Detroit Free Press* on July 6 carried a one-paragraph news item titled "Rumored Explosion." A similar story appeared that week in the *Detroit Daily Post*.

The papers told of a rumor circulating about the docks that the tug *Tawas* had exploded its boiler on Saginaw Bay. The *Free Press* said nothing more could be learned and that it was hoped the story wasn't true.

It wasn't true in July, 1871. The *Tawas*, however, did blow up three years later off Rock Falls, Michigan, not far from Saginaw Bay. Six crew members perished in the blast which destroyed the tug on May 14, 1874.

Was it a premonition of things to come? Did the newspaper get the story from someone who foretold the disaster three years early? The story originated from sailors at Port Huron. Did someone on a downbound ship have an unexplained vision and believe it really happened? The facts behind this strange coincidence may never be known.

On the Rocks

Cove Island
Georgian Bay
Thursday, July 6

The schooner *Castalia* was bound up Lake Huron, from Detroit to a lumber camp at Bying Inlet, Georgian Bay, when the vessel got too close to Cove Island Reef and came to a crashing stop on the rocks.

47

Although the *Castalia* didn't appear at first to be badly damaged, its position made salvage impossible. The boat came to rest in three feet of water, so far from deep water that tugs couldn't get close enough to pull it off. There was no cargo, the ship had no ballast and could not be made lighter. The hull was resting on solid rock and it was concluded that it would stay there. The vessel was stripped of its rigging, and then abandoned. Fishermen might still find remnants of the *Castalia* there today.

The *Castalia* was built at Sandusky, Ohio, in 1848, so had been in service 23 years.

Hot Tempers on the *Robert Emmett*

At Erie, Pa.
Saturday, July 15

Arguments happened among sailors while confined for weeks together aboard ship. They rarely got as serious as the fight between Capt. James Bradley and his mate, John Reed, on the schooner *Robert Emmett*.

The reason for the disagreement has long been forgotten. The two men apparently started their altercation while the *Emmett* was docked at Erie, unloading iron ore. They were still shouting angry words at one another while the ship was setting sail to start back up the lake. Later in the evening, the schooner returned to Erie harbor and dropped anchor. Reed came ashore in the yawl boat at 3:00 AM., Sunday, marched directly to the police station, and charged Captain Bradley with assaulting him with a knife. He told authorities that Bradley had chased him around the deck with a carving knife, and that he had defended himself by striking Bradley with a hand spike.

At about dawn the officers were accompanying Reed on their way to the *Emmett* to talk to Captain Bradley. Bradley met them on the dock. He was stepping ashore from the deck of a tug which brought him from his anchored schooner. Bradley was fuming. He said Reed took the ship's only small boat and left him stranded on the schooner. Once they saw one another, Bradley and Reed began their confrontation all over again. The police ended up arresting both men for disturbing the peace.

Bradley posted bail later in the day and filed charges against Reed. He said Reed committed assault, mutiny and stole the ship's boat. The case went to court on Monday. By then the story was circulating up and down the docks and the courtroom was packed with curious sailors . . many of them skippers of other vessels.

Justice of the Peace Foster found the two men still crazed with their anger and he was reluctant to get involved. He asked the captains in his courtroom if they would agree to settle the case through arbitration. The skippers said they wanted no part of this fight. How do you arbitrate with wild dogs, bent on killing one another?

Foster listened to a little testimony but then put an end to the matter. He found both Bradley and Reed guilty, fined them, and then ordered them both to pay court costs. Reed later was granted a court order to get his personal belongings off the *Emmett*.

Fire Aboard the *J. Barber*

On Lake Michigan
July 19

The porter, J. C. Nesbitt, took the blame for a fire that destroyed the steamer *J. Barber* on Lake Michigan during the early morning hours of July 19, 1871.

The official government report said the fire started from rags and towels hung by Nesbitt to dry near the smoke pipe. The report said the rags began burning and then dropped into the hold and into some pine slabs that the steamer was using for fuel. Nesbitt denied the charge. He said the wood in the casing around the smoke stack on the boiler deck was very dry. He said he had extinguished a small fire in the same place about three weeks earlier when the *Barber* was docked at Benton Harbor, Michigan.

The steamer was making a night trip from St. Joseph, Michigan, to Chicago when the fire broke out at about 12:30

AM. Its decks were laden with peaches, freshly picked the day before from Berrien County orchards. Only two passengers had booked passage that night.

The fire was discovered when the *Barber* was about thirty-five miles out in the lake. The sailors said the flames broke out on deck near the smoke stack after burning unchecked below for several minutes. Nesbitt and steward Harrie Wachter, who were sleeping in adjoining state rooms near the smoke stack, said they barely escaped alive. They said they were awakened when George Germain, the first mate, ran down the hallway shouting "fire." Both men tried to get dressed, but they said the fire progressed so fast they were driven from the cabin by smoke and flame before they found all their clothes.

The ship burned so fast there was no time to organize a fire fighting effort. Capt. James F. Snow ordered the engines stopped and told the officers and crew to lower the life boats. Wachter and Nesbitt said they were on the hurricane deck, helping in the launching of the boats, when fire broke through the wooden deck from the cabins below. They fled for their lives. When the life boats burned, Snow ordered tables, chairs, boards, doors and anything else that would float to be thrown overboard. He reasoned that survival would depend on having things to hang on to until help arrived.

The cook was seen using an ax to cut away some doors. When he jumped, his feet landed in the center of a floating door and he broke through to his waist. Wachter later remembered how comical it appeared. The man was not hurt and was using the door as if it were a life preserver. At the time, however, nobody was laughing. Wachter said flames lit the area as bright as daylight and he could see people clinging to wreckage all around him. Everybody was frightened.

Two crew members, watchman Pat Washington and deck hand Charles Brown were killed. They were not among the survivors and their bodies were never found after the fire consumed and then sank the steamer.

The fire served as a beacon in the night sky. Within twenty minutes, two steamers, the *Van Raalte* and *Corona*, arrived to pick up eighteen survivors. The propeller *Skylark*, which was steaming a few miles ahead of the *Barber*, also

Two crew members died when the *J. Barber* burned and sank on Lake Michigan.

saw the flames and turned around to help. The *Skylark* remained in the area until the next morning looking for the two missing sailors.

The *Sweeper*

The scow *Sweeper* was caught in a storm on Lake Michigan sometime around the middle of July. As the old ship rolled and twisted in the seas, the seams opened and the hold began filling with water. The crew manned the hand operated bilge pumps, but the water gained.

After several hours, the sailors tired and it was evident they were losing their fight to save the boat. The captain turned the vessel toward shore and grounded it near Waukegan, Illinois. The ship was full of tanning bark, which helped float the water logged vessel, even after water filled the hold. As soon as the boat hit land, the crew abandoned ship.

The captain went to Chicago and returned the next day on the tug *Louis Dole*, under command of Capt. William Crawford. The *Dole* pulled the scow back into deep water and then towed it to Chicago, where the hull was pumped out and repaired.

Saving the *Harvey Bissell*

On Lake Erie
Sunday, July 30

When the bark *Harvey Bissell* sprang a leak at the west end of Lake Erie, the crew experienced an endurance test at the pumps.

The ship was sailing from Toledo to Tonawanda with a load of lumber. The captain may have first thought he could finish the voyage if the crew could keep the hold from flooding. The *Bissell* was equipped with two Atlantic bilge pumps, the best available short of steam powered pumps, and the entire crew was taking turns working them. It was a bad leak because the water gained.

The tug *Kate Williams* arrived on the scene and took the *Bissell* in tow. Capt. J. Waltman, the skipper of the *Williams* turned the bark around and started a race to Detroit. The leak got worse. In spite of their efforts, the crew said the water was gaining about a foot every hour. Waltman ended up dragging the waterbound ship ashore at Point Pelee. He got it close enough so that when it sank, the *Bissell* was resting on the bottom in fourteen feet of water. Waltman steamed off to Detroit, where he picked up steam pumps and other equipment, then returned to salvage the *Bissell*.

The *Bissell* continued sailing the lakes until it stranded off False Presque Isle in 1905 and became a total loss. The ship was launched in 1866 at Toledo. It measured one hundred sixty-two feet, four inches in length.

Fire on the *Newhouse*

Grand Traverse Bay
Lake Michigan
Sunday, Aug. 6

It was thought that a kerosene lamp in the captain's cabin exploded, starting the fire that caused extensive damage to the lumber schooner *John S. Newhouse*.

It happened at 4:00 AM, somewhere off Grand Traverse Bay, not long after the captain left his quarters to walk out on deck. The fire spread so quickly the cook and second mate were trapped in adjoining quarters. Fellow crew members had to pull iron gratings away from the windows so they could escape. It was such a close call the cook had his hands and face blistered from the heat.

The sailors battled the fire all morning, but it spread to a cargo of lumber in the hold and burned out of control. The hull was flooded in an effort to snuff out the flames, causing the wooden schooner to be waterlogged. That afternoon the propeller *Susquehanna* saw the smoke, took off the crew, and tried to take the *Newhouse* in tow. The ship resisted the tow line. It turned on its beam ends and continued to float as a smoking hulk, half submerged in the water. The *Susquehanna* pulled it into Sutton's Bay until the wreck hit bottom.

The *Newhouse* was salvaged and repaired. It was built in Cleveland in 1836.

Opening the St. Clair Flats

Construction of the canal through the St. Clair Flats, at the mouth of the St. Clair River, was finished about August 1. The three hundred and sixty-five thousand dollar government project was part of the general plan to open navigation for larger ships from Duluth to Buffalo. It also was the first real channel built to help ships get through the shallow waters where the St. Clair River emptied into Lake St. Clair.

Before 1871, vessels chose the deepest of seven known passes. This was known as the north channel of the south pass. That waterway was deepened to eleven feet in 1858. The new canal opened shipping to bigger and heavier ships. According to a story in the *Detroit Free Press* on August 5, the canal was dug in three years by Canadian contractor John Brown. It measured three hundred feet in width, was eight thousand, four hundred and twenty-one feet long, and the water was eighteen feet deep. Most of the channel was protected by dikes and piers on both sides. Plans were already in the works to deepen the channel to twenty feet within the next twenty years.

The *Free Press* story noted, however, that the channel still had some shortcomings. For example, it said its three hundred foot width barely allowed two boats to pass each other without hitting. When a cross wind was blowing, there was great danger of collision.

Lumber haulers complained that the canal was going to be a tight squeeze for the big log rafts that they were towing down the river. The news story suggested that the rafts be steered through the old channel, which was shallow, but much wider.

The *Golden Fleece*

A decision by the U. S. Lighthouse Service to remove the revolving light from the Point aux Barques lighthouse, at the end of Lake Huron's Saginaw Bay, and replace it with a fixed light was not a good idea. Sailors knew two lights in the area, the one at the Port Austin Reef, a few miles west, and the Point aux Barques light, which was a point where downbound ships began their turn to the southeast to clear Michigan's small peninsula.

Before the light was changed, sailors knew the difference because the Point aux Barques light was always revolving, while the Port Austin light was fixed. When both lights were made to look alike, accidents started to happen.

The first recorded casualty was the three masted schooner *Golden Fleece,* which went aground on Port Austin Reef on August 6. The ship was laden with iron ore on its way down the lake from Escanaba. The crew mistook the light at Port Austin for Point aux Barques and steered directly into the reef.

The *Golden Fleece* was pulled off on August 14, after workers jettisoned two hundred tons of ore and then used a steam pump to get the water out of the hull. The schooner was towed to Detroit by the tug *McClellan* and repaired.

Lake Michigan Hardships

On Lake Michigan
Tuesday, Aug. 8

The sailors on the lumber scow *Forrest* scrambled when a gust of wind caught it broadside and the boat went over on her beam ends in stormy Lake Michigan. They said they felt the ship starting to tip and went to the taffrail to hang on as it rolled. Fortunately, the sails settled slowly into the water and the ship stayed afloat on its port side. Crew members said they were able to cut the ship's yawl boat free, bail it out, and then escape to shore.

The *Forrest* was on route from Muskegon, Michigan to Michigan City, Indiana with one hundred ten thousand feet of lumber when the storm swept down on it from the north northwest in the early morning hours. At first the ship ran well before the wind, but as the storm grew worse, the captain wanted to play it safe. He tried to turn the bow into the wind and drop anchor to ride out the storm in a time-honored way. In the *Forrest's* case, it was a mistake. As the scow was turning, a strong gust of wind caught the sails and the vessel capsized.

Two members of the crew, the cook and one deck hand, were caught below deck. They miraculously escaped. By the time they surfaced and grasped the floating hull, the other crew members had pulled away in the yawl boat. Either they forgot the two in their excitement, or else they never thought they could get out of the hull of the capsized vessel alive.

When someone looked back and saw the two men clinging to the wreck, the sailors tried to row the small boat back to get them. The battle against the wind was too much and the boat could make no headway. The stranded sailors on the wreck swam to the boat. After that, the crew spent about two days on the lake. They literally rowed their way to Chicago, arriving there at about 1:00 AM Saturday. The scow was towed into port by a passing steamer.

55

The *Scottish Chief*

On Lake Michigan
Tuesday, Aug. 8

The storm that capsized the *Forrest* also flooded the scow *Scottish Chief,* somewhere between Racine and Kenosha, Wisconsin. The ship took on water and became waterlogged and unmanageable by late Thursday afternoon. Even the galley was flooded as the ship floated in a partly submerged state. All of the food was ruined.

The sailors stayed with the wreck until Friday night, hoping that another ship would find them. When no help appeared, they abandoned ship. The crew spent another day and one-half in the open boat, arriving in Chicago on Sunday morning.

Demasting of the *Mary E. Perew*

On Lake Michigan
August 8

The bark *Mary E. Perew* was on the final leg of a trip from Lake Erie ports to Milwaukee with coal when the storm demasted it sixty miles west of the Manitou Islands.

Captain McNally said he saw the storm bearing down on the ship. He said the wind came on so fast that his men didn't have enough time to take in sails before it hit. The blast came with such a punch it snapped all three spars. The mizzen mast fell on the yawl boat, smashing it.

The *Perew* was left a floating derelict for nearly a week. McNally said his ship was demasted on Tuesday, and it wasn't taken in tow by the passing propeller *Montgomery* until the following Wednesday, August 14. The *Perew* apparently was well stocked with food and supplies so the crew fared all right. Nothing was told about hardships suffered during that long week of floating around on the lake. The *Montgomery* towed the bark into Milwaukee.

The bark *Mary E. Perew* floated at the mercy of the wind and sea for about a week after it was demasted.

Whatever Happened to the *Stella?*

Stories of a ship, floating upside down somewhere in the middle of Lake Michigan were told by skippers arriving in and out of the busy port of Chicago. Everyone first thought the sailors were seeing either the remains of the overturned scow *Forrest* or the *Scottish Chief.*

The reports continued and finally the tug *Caroline Williams* went out to find out if a fourth wreck, indeed, had occurred. The crew of the *Williams* made a terrible discovery on August 16. They came upon the floating hull of the schooner *Stella.* Captain J. M. Racmunson and two other unnamed men had sailed the *Stella* from Racine, Wisconsin to Pentwater, Michigan, at some undetermined time and never arrived. Racmunson and his men were presumed lost. But nobody was really sure what happened to them.

After the *Williams* brought the sixty-six-foot long vessel into Manistee, Michigan, an examination revealed even further mystery. While the ship showed what would have been normal damage from a catastrophe at sea . . . the cabin, masts and rigging were gone . . . it was discovered that the rigging had been purposefully removed. Marks on the stumps that had once been part of the schooner's masts showed that the spars were cut away with an ax. The sails, ropes, pulleys and even chains and anchors had been carefully removed from the wreck. Even the dead-eyes used to hold the ropes in place on key parts of the ship were removed.

Nobody knew what happened to the *Stella,* or its crew on that eventful trip. The ship was a new vessel, having just come out that year.

On the *John F. Ritchie*

On Lake Erie
Wednesday, Aug. 16

The captain of the lumber barge *John F. Ritchie* brought his wife, two other women, and several small children as guests on what was supposed to be a pleasant summer trip through the lakes. It turned out to be an experience in terror that no one would forget.

The *Ritchie* was one of a string of four lumber barges in tow behind the tug *Zonave,* hauling Michigan lumber from Bay City into Buffalo. After the vessels entered Lake Erie from the Detroit River on August 16, they encountered a freak storm. It blew so hard and strong, the *Ritchie* broke away from its tow line and was cast adrift.

As the women and children huddled together in the cabin, the waves crashed over the deck of the helpless ship. The deck load of lumber broke loose and slid overboard with a terrible noise. The cabin began to creak and groan under the force of the waves, and it was feared that the storm might carry it away. The crew led the women and children out of the only shelter they had and lashed them to the mast on the open deck. The cabin indeed washed away, carrying with it all of the clothes and personal belongings of the guests and crew. The ship's hold filled with water, turning the *Ritchie* into a waterlogged wreck, partly submerged and at the mercy of the storm.

It was a miracle that the ship and its passengers survived. The next day, a passing steamer came upon the wreck, took everybody aboard, and towed the *Ritchie* into Cleveland. The leaky barge sank at the Cleveland dock.

Capsizing of the *Winfield Scott*

At Deaths Door
Lake Michigan
Thursday, Aug. 17

The crew of the schooner *Winfield Scott* was miraculously saved after the ship capsized in heavy seas near Deaths Door, the entrance to Green Bay. The sailors clung to the wreckage of the overturned vessel from Thursday night until noon Friday before they were rescued by the schooner *Ethan Allen.*

The *Scott,* under command of Capt. Harry Faith, left Menominee, Michigan Thursday morning with a load of lumber, bound for Chicago. The schooner tacked its way northeast across Green Bay against a brisk southeast wind, then encountered heavy seas that evening at the entrance to Lake Michigan.

The boat labored in those seas until Spider Island was sighted. By then, the wind was strengthening into a gale and Faith called up the watch to take in the head canvas. The crew struggled against the wind and the cold spray from the seas breaking over the bow as they secured the flying jib, the jib stay-sail and foresail. When Faith was satisfied, the sailors went back to the forecastle, only to discover that it was filling with water. The ship had developed a bad leak and was almost sunk.

Even before he learned of the problem, Faith was sensing that something was wrong. He said the boat was getting sluggish in the water and hard to manage. He ordered the mainsail double reefed, but before the sailors got the job done, the schooner broached awkwardly in a sea and went over on its beam ends.

The sailors thought they went in the water at about 11:00 PM. They hung on the wreck about thirteen hours before the *Ethan Allen* came along. The *Scott* drifted aground on Spider Island and probably broke up. There is no record of salvage.

Grounding of the *Pierrepont*

On Lake Huron
Saturday, Aug. 19

The schooner *Pierrepont* was struggling against a heavy southeastern gale, making its way from Detroit to Silver Island, Lake Superior, with coal and lime when it went aground near the Detour lighthouse, at the north end of Lake Huron, and filled with water. The crew got safely away, but the *Pierrepont's* timbers took a terrible pounding. The sails, ropes and pulleys were removed and the vessel was abandoned by her owners.

The *Pierrepont* wasn't finished. The wrecking tug *Leviathan* had the hull raised and delivered to a Port Huron dry dock ten days later. They said the keel was mostly gone, and there were several holes in her hull. The boat was rebuilt and put back on the lakes.

The *Pierrepont* was built at Sackett's Harbor in 1852, which made it nineteen years old at the time of the grounding.

Burning of the *Akron*

Ogdensburgh, N.Y.
Saturday, Aug. 19

While the *Pierrepont* was pounding on the northern end of Lake Huron, the steamer *Akron* was burning at the wharves of Ogdensburgh, on the St. Lawrence River.

Details of the fire are sketchy. The steamer arrived in port at about 9:00 PM, the fires were drawn from the furnaces and the crew turned in for the night. At about midnight the night watch discovered a fire in the ship's hold. The cause of the fire was never learned.

The crew scuttled the ship to put the fire out and save both the *Akron* and its cargo. The boat later was raised and repaired.

Ramming the *Spy*

On Lake Michigan
Monday, Aug. 21

The schooners *Spy* and *J. V. Taylor* collided on Lake Michigan, somewhere off Waukegan, Illinois, at about midnight. The *Spy* was hit broadside and suffered extensive damage. The damaged boat, with Capt. W. F. Mitchell at the helm, was traveling light from Chicago to Sheboygan, while the *Taylor* was sailing toward Chicago with a load of lumber.

The *Taylor* hit the *Spy* on the port side. The crash cracked the Spy's hull, carried away the rail and stanchions, damaged the main mast, and tore out much rigging and sail. Damage was estimated at over two thousand dollars.

Raising the *Cromwell*

At the Straits of Mackinaw
Saturday, Aug. 26

The recovery of the sunken Canadian steamer *Oliver Cromwell* by the Boston Wrecking Co. was a most remarkable event. The *Cromwell* had laid a sunken and an almost forgotten wreck at the Straits of Mackinaw following a collision with the schooner *Jessie* in October, 1857, fourteen years earlier!

The wreck was found to be in such good condition that J. P. Clark, the Detroit man who purchased claims to it, said he would restore the boat and put it back into service. Even the machinery in the flooded engine room was found to be in good condition.

The reason for Clark's interest in the old wreck is unclear. For some unexplained reason he financed a six-week-long salvage operation led by a Captain Falcon, who developed a way to successfully pull the old wreck out of the mud and bring it to the surface. To do it, Falcon sent divers down with water filled, air-tight casks, which were attached to the side of the wreck with large eye-bolts. A chain was passed through the eye-bolts, until it circled the ship, holding everything together. When all was ready, air was pumped into the casks. This process continued for several days. On August 26 the massive hulk rose out of the mud and lifted to the surface. One newspaper reporter, among the many spectators attracted to the scene in private vessels that day, described the event: "Murmuring, bubbling sounds were heard. The waters above the rising mass were lifted higher and higher, and they were deeply tinged with mud and sediment. Numbers of dead and stunned fish were continually popping to the surface, and small water spouts were shooting out in all directions. . . . . Then, bubbling and spouting like a seething cauldron, out shot the huge monster, first the stern and then the bow as if by magic from below."

The wreck was, at first look, an ugly thing to see. Its upper cabin was missing and the main deck broken. The *Cromwell* still displayed the damage to its side that sank it fourteen years earlier. The wreck smelled of the lake bottom and fish. After a while, the smell of rotted cargo . . . wheat, flour and salt pork . . . began reaching the nostrils of the onlookers. As stated above, the boat was in unusually good condition after such a long time on the bottom. There was still paint on the engine, and mechanics found that the pistons were still oiled and in working condition. The wheel was still in place. A clock was found stopped at 12:40 o'clock, believed to have been the hour of the sinking. There were no human skeletons. The crew had escaped safely in a small boat.

The tugs *Islander* and *Grace Dormer* towed the wreck to Mackinaw City, where it was moored for a while. While there, the wreck became a magnet, drawing sightseers from miles around. Clark kept his promise and restored the *Cromwell* to lake service, although it never moved again under its own power. The engines were removed, the hull restored, and the ship was used as a tow barge.

Rough Weather on Lake Erie

Sailors say that Lake Erie is one of the worst places to be caught when the wind blows hard. Erie is only two hundred and ten feet at its deepest point, making it the shallowest of all the Great Lakes. Sudden storms can whip the lake into a frenzy in minutes. The month of September 1871 opened with at least two hearty blows, causing lots of trouble on Erie.

A northeaster that developed during the night of Wednesday, September 6, wrecked the coal laden schooner *Rosa Stearns* at Cleveland. After battling the storm for hours, the boat was approaching Cleveland's harbor. Instead of finding safety, the ship was driven into the stone pier and smashed to pieces at about 1:00 AM. To save themselves, the crew jumped to the pier and then crawled ashore, grabbing the wet boulders and hanging on as the waves crashed over their heads.

The fore and aft schooner *Morning Light* was sailing from Kelley's Island with a cargo of stone for Marquette, Michigan, when it got caught in another blow on the morning of Friday, September 8, at the west end of Lake Erie. The crew tried to make the mouth of the Detroit River, miscalculated their position, and ran the ship aground on Point Moullier, just below Gibralter. The ship hit a sandy bottom, and the men scuttled the *Morning Light* to save it from harm. The steamer *Hurt,* under command of a Captain McFarlane, spotted the wreck the following day, reported it at Detroit, and the tug *George N. Brady* was sent out with steam pumps and hawsers to salvage it.

The schooner *New Lisbon* wasn't as lucky. It capsized in the September 8 storm off Fairport, Ohio. The crew was picked up the same day by the propeller *Annie Young.* The *Young* then steamed off for Detroit, leaving the partly submerged schooner drifting off with its cargo of wooden staves. Staves already could be seen floating out of the hold of the overturned ship and into the lake. The wreck was reported still floating on its beam ends about a week later by the brig *Helfenstein* so a tug from Cleveland made an attempt to find it. The search turned up nothing. On September 16, eight days later, the bark *Jennie P. Mack* came upon the wreck, still floating upside down between Fairport and Ashtabula, and took it in tow. By the time it reached port the *New Lisbon's* hull was split and the boat was written off as a total loss.

Mutiny on the *Moss*

Cleveland, Ohio
Saturday, Sept. 9

The incident was called a mutiny, but that wasn't quite the right word. The captain of the schooner *A. H. Moss,* a man named Hicks, provoked his crew to wrath the day he lost his temper and fired his mate.

It turned out that the unidentified mate was popular with the men while Captain Hicks was not admired by anyone. The mate left the ship moments before a tug began to tow the schooner out of Cleveland harbor. The men chose that moment to go on strike.

When the tow line was cast off and Captain Hicks ordered the sailors to hoist sail, he discovered the rebellion. Nobody would do any work. The *Moss* floated around for a while and nothing happened. People on shore saw the ship out there and began remarking about the strangeness of what it was doing . . . or better said, was not doing.

Out of desperation, Hicks raised signal flags and had a tug tow his vessel back into the harbor. When the *Moss* dropped anchor there on Sunday morning, he fired the entire crew and went ashore to hire another. It wasn't the first strike by sailors in Great Lakes history, but it was among the most spontaneous.

Trouble With Smoke

Smoke from forest fires in Michigan, Wisconsin and northern Ohio was becoming a serious problem to ships by mid-September. It had been an extra dry summer and the forests were burning all around the Great Lakes. On certain days the smoke hung like fog, making navigation difficult even in broad daylight. It caused several accidents.

The bark *Sunrise* went ashore on the Canadian side of lower Lake Huron, eight miles above Port Edward, Ontario, sometime around September 9. The *Sunrise* was headed down the lake with wheat and was trying to make the St. Clair River when the accident happened. When it hit the rocky coast, the bark put a hole in its bottom, causing the holds full of grain to flood. After a time the wheat started to swell, putting pressure on the wooden hull. Before salvagers could get to the boat, the hull split open. The *Sunrise* was a total loss.

Another casualty of the smoke was the propeller *Annie Young,* which was steaming up the Detroit River after having rescued the crew of the capsized schooner *New Lisbon* on Lake Erie (See Rough Weather on Lake Erie). The *Annie Young's* pilot was blinded by smoke and the boat went aground on Fighting Island on Sunday, September 10. It was pulled free a few days later and continued its journey to Detroit.

By Tuesday, September 12, the smoke was so heavy it was causing captains to drop anchor rather than risk their ships. The master of the steamer *W. R. Clinton* dispatched a telegram to the ship's owners from one Lake Huron port in which he said the vessel was delayed twelve hours.

A story in a Detroit newspaper said thirty-eight ships and four strings of barges in tow were anchored at Point au Pellee, on Lake Erie, on September 12, waiting for the smoke to lift.

Mid-river Crash

The downbound grain-laden barkentine *J. G. Masten* collided with the schooner *Maid of the Mist* in the early morning of September 10, 1871, on the St. Clair River, just below the Port Huron town limits. The *Masten's* skipper, Capt. James Kendrick was blamed for the accident because his ship hit the *Maid of the Mist* while it was anchored for the night on the river. A judge ruled that the barkentine was traveling too fast.

Kendrick said he was standing forward on the *Masten's* deck when the schooner was noticed about one hundred feet ahead at about 2:00 AM. He said he ordered the wheelsman to turn hard starboard, but it was too late. The bow of the *Masten* struck the schooner on the starboard side, carrying away its jib boom, head gear and foremast head, breaking the starboard stanchions and driving the *Masten's* anchor through the side of the hull. The schooner sank about ninety minutes later. By then Capt. John Jones and the four members of his crew had time to abandon ship. Kendrick said the *Masten* was traveling about six miles an hour after entering the headwaters of the river from Lake Huron, and his crew was taking in sail even when the accident happened. He said he was standing forward near the lookout when the anchored schooner was spotted dead ahead. Both Kendrick and the lookout, George Johnson, testified that they saw no lights on the *Maid of the Mist.*

A court of inquiry at Detroit awarded damages to the owners of the *Maid of the Mist.* Not only was the bark traveling recklessly, but the court said its crew failed to see the lights of the anchored schooner before it was too late. The court believed Jones when he said the lamps were lit and hanging in their proper place.

Look Ma, No Rudder!

Detroit, Mich.
Tuesday, Sept. 10

A strange story appeared in the *Detroit Free Press* about the Canadian tug *Jessie,* which tore its rudder in shallows while towing barges from Chatham, Ontario, on the Detroit River to Buffalo.

The captain, who was not named, decided to keep his schedule and brought the rudderless ship and its consorts down the river to Detroit before stopping for repair. How he accomplished this bit of seamanship without a way to steer his ship was never explained. Maybe it helped that he was traveling down stream. The story said the *Jessie* had to be helped into dry dock by other tugs after it reached Detroit.

Seeing a Ghost

Port Stanley, Ont.
Tuesday, Sept. 10

Port authorities and dock workers stared in disbelief when the scow *Dunham* sailed into the harbor. The boat had been written off as lost on Lake Erie following a bad storm that caught it twenty-two days earlier during a trip to Port Stanley from Cleveland. When the *Dunham* didn't arrive, and then failed to report anywhere else along the lake that week, people assumed it sank and that all hands were drowned. Families were notified. The crew was being mourned as dead and lost.

The acting skipper of the *Dunham,* a man named Wright, had been elevated from the rank of first mate. He explained how the ship got caught in a bad southeast gale after sailing from Cleveland with a load of coal on August 19. The scow rolled wildly in the seas, and after developing a leak, Wright turned around and ran before the wind. Instead of sailing northeast toward Port Stanley, the *Dunham* traveled west, northwest to the cluster of islands off Port Clinton, Ohio. Here the ship ducked to the lee of one of the islands, dropped anchor and rode out the storm.

Wright couldn't explain why it took him so long to bring the *Dunham* back to Port Stanley once the storm was over.

The Killing

Detroit, Mich.
Sunday, Sept. 10

There was bad blood.

That wasn't unusual among sailors. The very nature of the profession . . . if we can call the dangerous work of running a ship on the Great Lakes in 1871 a profession . . . drew coarse types of men who were sometimes quick to anger. They were, generally, an unknown people, coming and going at various ports of call. When ships sank, their names sometimes were not on the roster. They would be remembered as "Joe from Toledo," but little else known. Thus it was when trouble erupted aboard the steamer *Milton D. Ward* that Sunday, nobody gave it a lot of thought.

It was a serious enough incident, though, to get seaman Andrew W. Williamson fired. When the *Ward* tied up at Detroit on September 10, Williamson was given his pay and sent packing. He left the ship but he didn't leave the area. Williamson stayed around the wharf, mixing with the crowd,

The Steamer *Milton D. Ward* was the scene of a bloody stabbing while docked at Detroit.

stopping at the local saloons, mixing alcohol with his anger. That evening, when some of the crew members were given free time in port, Williamson was there to encounter his old nemesis, sailor David Solemund, in a local bar. Williamson's eyes were red from his many hours of drinking. His face was flushed from the heat of his anger. The men met face-to face and exchanged angry words. They stepped out on the street where Solemund, having the advantage of sobriety, duked it out with the troublesome Williamson. Solemund won the fight fair and square, leaving Williamson lying bloodied and flat in the dust. By now Williamson's anger was out of control. He swore that he would return and cut Solemund's heart out. Solemund and his friends laughed off the threat and left.

The *Ward* was scheduled to leave port at midnight, so the crew was back on board early that evening, getting the ship ready for the trip. A few minutes before midnight, Williamson's gray shadow crossed the wharf. He slipped down the gangway, walked directly up to Solemund, and before anyone could react, he stabbed the man twice in the chest and fled. Solemund died in a pool of blood. The knife was driven deep in his heart.

Detroit police arrested the thirty-six-year-old Williamson at Matt Van Courtland's boarding house. They found him in bed. He wasn't asleep. He was just lying there, his eyes open, staring at the ceiling. During an inquest a day or two later, it was learned that both Solemund and Williamson took jobs aboard the *Ward* at the same time, only a week before the killing. They knew each other, bunked together, and appeared to have once been friends.

The Blow of September 13

Two boats came on hard times when they were caught in a storm that swept the lakes on September 13.

The schooner *W. H. Vanderbilt* went aground on Lake Michigan near Grosse Point, about twelve miles north of Chicago, with thirty-five thousand bushels of wheat stowed in the hold. The wreck happened at about 2:00 AM. By the time Captain Crawford brought the tug *George W. Wood* to the scene he found a haggard crew busy dumping sacks of wheat overboard in an effort to save their ship. One look at the *Vanderbilt* told Crawford that it would take more than simple lightening to refloat that boat. The *Vanderbilt* was lying broadside on, its deck tilted at a strange, unnatural angle. Crawford took the crew aboard his tug and returned to Chicago to wait until the storm died. The *Vanderbilt* later was salvaged successfully.

On Lake Erie, the steamer *Jacques Cartier,* under command of the owner, Capt. George Coveyau, was carrying a load of barrel staves from Detroit to Buffalo when the storm struck. Off Cleveland, the seas swept the *Cartier's* decks with such force, the ship's cabin and upper works were smashed. The ship flooded and disaster seemed eminent by the time a tug arrived to take the stricken vessel in tow. Coveyau was operating on such a close margin the storm ruined him. He was forced to sell the *Cartier* at a portion of its value to pay off his debts.

Mystery Deaths

Menominee, Mich.
On Green Bay
Wednesday, Sept. 13

The same storm that wrecked the *Vanderbilt* and *Cartier* may have been responsible for the strange drownings of four sailors from the bark *S. D. Pomeroy* while it was anchored off Menominee.

Archie Dickie, James Steele, John Davidson and James Merchie were last seen alive in the ship's yawl, rowing their way toward shore. The yawl drifted ashore empty. People said the boat was right side up and dry when it came in. The bodies of all four men floated ashore later in the day.

Nobody could explain how all four sailors could have fallen from the yawl at the same time if the boat wasn't tipped or swamped by a wave.

Sinking of the *Union*

On Lake Michigan
Sunday, Sept. 17

The schooner *Union* developed a leak while sailing from Sheboygan, Wisconsin to Manistee, Michigan, with a cargo of thirty-two thousand bricks. Water was discovered in the hold at 2:30 AM when the ship was twenty-five miles out of Sheboygan. In spite of efforts to save the boat, the heavily laden *Union* settled lower and lower in the water. The crew abandoned ship moments before it sank. The sailors were picked up at 9:00 AM by a passing scow on its way to Chicago.

The *Jay Gould* almost cut the steamer *Dictator* in half when the boats collided at South Manitou Island.

Wrecked at the Dock

South Manitou Island
Lake Michigan
Sunday, Sept. 17

The propeller *Dictator* was moored for a brief stop at South Manitou Island on Sunday morning when an unexpected disaster struck. The steamer *Jay Gould* came too fast into the harbor, rammed the *Dictator* broadside, cutting the ship almost in two and turning it violently around. The *Dictator* sank with its bow in about thirty feet of water and the stern resting high and dry on the shore. The crew apparently escaped injury.

The *Dictator's* cargo of seventeen thousand bushels of barley and some of its deckload of flour was salvaged. The ship was refloated in October after weeks of work by the Coast Wrecking Company tug *Rescue*. By the time the *Dictator* rested in dry dock, a series of early autumn storms made a mark on the wreck. The upper cabins were nearly demolished. The *Gould* was not damaged.

The *Dictator* was bound down the lakes that day from Chicago to Buffalo, and had stopped at Racine and Milwaukee to take on cargo. The ship was built at Buffalo in 1863.

Lost *Miranda*

There are two different stories about what happened to the schooner *Miranda*. Neither story could be confirmed nor denied. Yet they are so different, it makes one wonder if there weren't two schooners by the same name that met their end at the same time, on different lakes.

The ship was wrecked sometime in mid-September. Beer's *History of the Great Lakes* claims there was one *Miranda* and that it was wrecked in 1871 near Point aux Barques, off Lake Huron's Saginaw Bay. The story, also told in Michigan newspapers of the day, claimed that the *Miranda* was a wood hauler, engaged in the lumber trade between Saginaw Valley and Buffalo.

The basic story goes like this: The *Miranda* was downbound with a load of lumber when it lost its way in smoke from a Michigan forest fire one night and went aground on Port Austin Reef. The crew claimed it mistook the Port Austin light for the light at Point aux Barques, a few miles to the east, and didn't realize they were coming up on the reef. Before help arrived the twenty-three-year-old ship broke up and was a total loss. The crew escaped. The owners stripped the vessel and abandoned it.

Story number two is more haunting. It appeared in the *Detroit Daily Post* on September 28: The *Miranda* was found by a passing ship in a waterlogged condition, half submerged, off Michigan City, Indiana, on Lake Michigan. The boat's hold was filled with railroad ties. The crew of the unknown vessel noticed the lifeboat was still in the davits and decided to search the cabins. There they made a gruesome discovery. The drowned bodies of an elderly man and a boy of about seventeen were found floating in the partly flooded room. A clock was found that had stopped at twelve o'clock.

Sunk on the Detroit River

Windsor, Ont.
Sept. 20

The river steamer *George Jerome* sank in twenty-five feet of water after the ferry *Detroit* clipped its stern as both vessels approached the Windsor dock. Both boats were crossing the river from Detroit at about 11:00 PM. The *Jerome* got in front of the *Detroit's* bow and the ferry overran the smaller steamer. The *Jerome* immediately filled and sank. Two of the four crew members jumped aboard the ferry and two others found themselves in the river. They were rescued by a small boat from the *Detroit*.

Wreck of the *C. H. Hurd*

On Northern Lake Michigan
Friday, Sept. 22

Captain W. O. Harrison was the only survivor after his ship, the three masted schooner *C. H. Hurd,* foundered in a storm about three miles off the head of South Manitou Island. He drifted ashore on North Manitou Island, still clinging to wreckage, the following afternoon.

The body of Harrison's wife washed up on the island on Sunday. Also lost with the ship were Harrison's young son, his brother, Sidney M. Harrison, first mate; Christian Oleson, second mate; and J. Babcock, the cook. Four other unnamed sailors also perished.

Harrison said the *Hurd* left Chicago on Thursday night with twenty-eight thousand bushels of corn, bound for Buffalo. A violent southwesterly gale developed Friday as the schooner was making its way to the north end of Lake Michigan.

Harrison's personal story, printed September 28 in the *Detroit Daily Tribune,* was graphic: "When the dog watch was called at 4:00 PM, the vessel was under very short sail. We were running away from mountain high seas coming at her from astern. We had to keep sail enough to drive her ahead of those seas. All three hatches were secure. They were double battened down with double tarpaulins and were water tight," he said.

At about 6:00 PM, just after supper, when three miles south-southwest of South Manitou Island, he said the ship was swept by an unusually large sea that flooded the deck, carrying away everything not lashed down. Harrison said the wave wrenched the yawl boat from its davits at the stern and swept it forward across the open deck. He thought some of the crew members on the deck were swept overboard by the wave and wayward boat.

He explained that because the ship was deep loaded, it was "already down to the plank shear so that when this sea came aboard its weight sank her down until the scuppers and the lower part of the bulwarks were completely under water. The pressure of the water outside the scuppers being greater than inside prevented the water from escaping. The schooner was thus held down while sea after sea swept over her. One of them lifted the whole top part of the after cabin and washed it overboard. The water then rushed into the cabin and from there found its way into the hold. The forecastle scuttle was also washed away, and water started entering the hold by that means.

Harrison said a new squall turned the boat, causing her to labor heavily. "I was standing the wheel with one of the sailors and had given orders to settle away the mainsail to ease the vessel when another heavy sea rolled over her." This wave carried both Harrison and the other sailor overboard at the same moment. "I saved myself by catching hold of the reef tackle fall of the main boom, which was hanging over the side, and succeeded in crawling myself on deck. The other man went down.

"I had previously instructed the mate, my brother, to take my wife and child up into the mizzen rigging, saying I would take care of the schooner. When I got back aboard, I saw him with my wife and child in the mizzen top. The men had now also taken to the rigging, and seeing that the vessel was rapidly filling and going down, I threw off my coat, hat and boots, and prepared for the worst."

Harrison said he was also climbing into the rigging when the ship sank with a lurch, taking with it the crew and the captain's family. Harrison went down with the ship too, but somehow broke away. Because he had pealed off his heavy clothing just moments before, he managed to swim back to the surface before he drowned. "I was under water a very long time, and when my breath was almost gone, I reached the surface."

He said he climbed on a piece of the cabin roof, and grabbed an iron ring he found attached to it. "In this way I continued for eleven hours . . . there was on the roof an overcoat and I held onto it in one hand, waiting for an opportunity to put it on, while still clinging to the iron ring."

Every time a wave rushed over him, Harrison said he shut his eyes and held his breath. "After midnight the wind lulled somewhat and enabled me to throw the overcoat over my shoulders, although I was so numb as scarcely to be able to move." He said he began kicking his feet and striking the raft with a small piece of wood, just to stay awake and keep his circulation going. "About daylight, being by then entirely exhausted, I came in sight of land, which proved to be the southwest end of North Manitou Island. Shortly after that the raft was landed on the beach." He said he used sticks as canes and worked his way for two and one-half miles along the beach to the home of the lighthouse keeper, a Captain Pickard.

The *Hurd* was built in Detroit in 1868 so was a relatively new ship. It measured five hundred and seventy-seven tons.

Strange Occurrence at Port Sanilac

Port Sanilac, Mich.
Wednesday, Sept. 27

The people of Port Sanilac were abuzz. A strange dark ship. . . identified only as a bark rigged sailing ship with dark sails, had been anchored off that port for nearly a week and nobody knew why. Rumors were flying. People were saying that the men aboard this strange ship tossed about a hundred barrels of pork, butter and lard overboard and were waiting for it to wash ashore. Others said they knew for a fact that the crew was stricken with small pox.

Fishing boats dared to draw close to look at the stranger. Attempts to hail the crew and learn the purpose of the long visit met with silence, the stories said. Nobody dared to board the mystery ship and confront the unknown. They didn't even get its name. Every day brought wilder and wilder stories.

One day the strange vessel disappeared. It sailed off into the night as mysteriously and as unannounced as it arrived.

Burning of the *Nebraska*

Chicago, Ill.
Thursday, Sept. 28

The fire started somewhere in the engine room on the new propeller *Nebraska* while it was moored at the Galena grain terminal dock, taking on a load of grain. The steamer, under the command of Capt. Nicholas Gebhard, had been docked there since Wednesday night and already had thirty-nine thousand bushels of wheat and oats, and a hundred bags of flour stowed away in the hold.

The fire was discovered by a customs house inspector at 1:40 AM. Most of the ship's crew of about thirty people were caught asleep in the forecastle, located at the bow. Because the fire was at the aft end of the ship, crew members had time to escape with their clothes and baggage.

Captain Gebhard, who was staying ashore that night, arrived at the dock and learned that nobody thought to rescue his trunk and the ship's papers. People were surprised when the forty-seven-year-old veteran sailor climbed over the side of the burning ship, entered his smoke-filled cabin and salvaged his things.

Chicago fire fighters fought the blaze for hours, but could not save the ship and cargo from extensive damage. At one point, the flames reached the wooden superstructure and it burned with such heat the nearby elevator was threatened.

Had it not been contained, the great Chicago fire might have occurred about a week earlier than it did.

Gebhard, who had interests in the *Nebraska* along with Buffalo owners, announced plans to rebuild her. It was fortunate that they decided to have the ship towed to Buffalo before the Chicago fires began. The *Nebraska* was a survivor. Many other vessels caught in the harbor that week were consumed by the fire.

The *Nebraska* was one of the giant carriers of its day, especially designed as a freight hauler on the run between Chicago and Buffalo. It measured two hundred and nineteen feet in length and had a capacity of fifteen hundred tons. The ship continued sailing the lakes as the *Nebraska,* and later as a lumber carrier under the name *Congress* until 1904, when it caught fire and burned again off South Manitou Island. The second fire destroyed the boat.

The *Nebraska* **caught fire at Chicago a few days before the city was destroyed by a mystery blaze.**

FALL

Smoke Got in Their Eyes

On Lake Huron
Point aux Barques, Mich.
Monday, Oct. 2

Smoke from forest fires in the upper midwest had been affecting shipping for at least a month. By this date the problem was intensifying.

The fore and aft schooner *Montezuma* was among the casualties during the first week in October. This boat was sunk about forty miles above Point aux Barques when it was hit broadside by the schooner *Hattie Johnston* in "thick weather" during the early hours of the day. Both vessels claim to have been well lighted, but crews failed to see one another because of smoke.

The bow of the *Johnston* struck the *Montezuma* just forward the main sail with such force it nearly cut the vessel's wooden hull in two. The crew of the ill-fated *Montezuma* abandoned ship in life boats. Some jumped over the rail to the *Johnston* while the two boats were still embraced and their sails and rigging tangled. Sailors had to cut away the rigging with great haste to free the *Johnston* as the other ship settled, its weight threatening to capsize the *Johnston*. Within the hour the *Montezuma* capsized and sank. The *Johnston* took so much damage that it was unable to get to port without help. The vessel dropped anchor and waited for another ship to come along and take her in tow.

The *Montezuma* was downbound with more than sixteen thousand bushels of corn bound for Buffalo.

78

Other shipwrecks that week:

➥ The Union Steamship Line's propeller *W. M. Tweed* ran aground on Sugar Island, near Thunder Bay Light, late on Tuesday, October 3, the night after the *Montezuma's* sinking. The ship was heavy laden with freight, including a deck load of railroad iron, when it hit. The *Tweed* was pulled free a week later by the tugs *Prindiville* and *M. I. Mills*.

➥ The schooner *E. B. Allen* went ashore the night of October 3 just north of Frankfort, Michigan. This vessel was carrying a cargo of wheat from Chicago. A tug later pulled it free.

➥ The schooner *H. S. Fairchilds* was sunk following a collision with the schooner *Harvest Home* on Friday night, October 6, off Lake Erie's Long Point. The *Home* was bound up while the *Fairchilds* was downbound with nearly twenty thousand bushels of wheat from Milwaukee. The *Fairchilds* sank quickly in deep water, and the crew escaped without injury. Heavy smoke was again blamed. The *Fairchilds* was built at Rochester, New York in 1857.

➥ The steamer *Wyoming* went ashore sometime that week near Forester, Michigan, on Lake Huron. Heavy smoke was blamed. The boat was reportedly still there the night of the big storm and forest fires on Sunday, October 8, but details are sketchy. The ship is not listed as a casualty that fall.

➥ The bark *Major Anderson* also went ashore that week in heavy smoke at Two Rivers, Michigan. The *Anderson* later broke up and was destroyed.

➥ The schooner *Melvina,* bound up with coal, went aground in dense smoke on Lake Erie's Clay Banks on Saturday, October 7. The tug *Quayle* found it there and went to Detroit for pumps and hawsers to pull it free.

➥ That same day the propellers *Wenona* and *Empire State* went aground in the St. Clair Flats while trying to get into the St. Clair River from Lake St. Clair. Tugs pulled the two vessels free again.

➥ The schooner *Gem* sprang a leak on Lake Erie and sank in shallow water off Pigeon Point. The *Gem* went down during "thick weather" on Saturday, October 7.

The *Navarino* was among the fleet of boats that burned during the great Chicago Fire.

The Burning of Everything

The fall of 1871 is remembered in the upper midwest as the time of the great holocaust. While the City of Chicago was ablaze on the night of Sunday, October 8, fires fanned by strong westerly winds also were sweeping the ultra-parched forests of Wisconsin, Illinois, Michigan, Minnesota and Ohio.

It was a time of black horror for thousands of people trapped in the forests. Some who lived near the coast of the Great Lakes, or near the myriad of small lakes and streams that dot the landscape, tried to outrun the fire, hoping to escape to the safety of the water. Some sought shelter in their shallow dug wells. Others determined to stand and fight to save their homes and their towns. They were doing all of these things when they died. Few had a chance as the flames, fanned by a gale force wind, swept down on them without mercy. Some miraculously survived.

No one is quite sure how many people perished. The numbers in large tracts across Michigan and Wisconsin were relatively low because people were only just beginning to clear and settle this part of the country. Elsewhere, entire towns were leveled. Hundreds, perhaps thousands of people stumbled out of the smoke badly burned, lacking food, shelter and clothing.

The Chicago fire was so terrible the story overwhelmed news of the other fires burning at the same time in at least five other states. Even to this day, history books fail to mention or else lightly touch on the other fires, even though they were believed to have burned more square miles and done more property damage than any other single conflagration in American history. No disaster of that magnitude has been experienced in the United States before or since.

The fires had a profound effect on the ships plying the lakes. As Chicago burned, many fine vessels were destroyed there. They included the new propeller *Navarino,* schooner *Glenbula,* schooner *Eclipse,* schooner *Butcher Boy,* bark *Valetta,* schooner *Alewick,* bark *A. P. Nichols,* bark *Fontanella,* fore and aft schooner *Stampede,* schooner *N. C. Ford,* and schooner *Christina Nielson.* The only recorded casualties among sailors occurred on the *Alewick,* where the mate was said to have died and the captain suffered severe burns to his hands.

The iron clad propeller *Merchant* was moored at Chicago, but the crew got up steam and the boat escaped before the fire claimed it.

Elsewhere, the schooner *Seneca Chief* was destroyed in a fire at Manistee, Michigan. It was one of several vessels tied up at docks on the Manistee River when fire swept the entire city, burning more than a hundred homes and most businesses. Other boats, including the tug *Bismark,* with three barges in tow, and a scow loaded with slabs and a pile driver, escaped into Lake Michigan.

Historians have theorized that some common abnormal event sparked those great conflagrations. Ideas have ranged from severe lightning storms to a meteor shower. Author Mel Waskin suggested in his book, *Mrs. O'Leary's Comet,* that a comet collided with the earth and fiery parts of it hit Chicago, Wisconsin and Western Michigan. Waskin suggests that the fire was too hot to be a normal fire. There is support to the theory. Survivors of both the fires at Chicago and Peshtigo, Wisconsin, told how everything became so hot that strange things happened. The iron railroad tracks at Peshtigo, for example, became bent and twisted by the flames. Attempts by fire fighters in Chicago to stop the advance of the flames became futile because the fire seemed to jump hundreds of feet through the air from one building to another; sometimes crossing rivers and open fields.

There are some statistics that don't support Waskin's theory. Newspaper accounts told of fires already burning in the woods in various parts of Michigan during September and even as early as August. A story in the *Detroit Daily Post* on October 5 told of fires sweeping the forests in northern Ohio, destroying houses and corn fields near New Haven. The story said the Toledo, Wabash and Western Railroad was forced to stop running trains because of the fires. Fires also were said to have been raging out of control in the forests of Wisconsin and even across the western prairies of Minnesota on October 4. An estimated one hundred families in the northeastern counties of Wisconsin were said to have been escaping to Green Bay as the fires destroyed their homes. Wild animals and even bears were witnessed fleeing across open fields.

There had been little rain, the summer had been unusually hot and the forests were dry and combustible. As already recorded, smoke was a common problem on the lakes long before the events of October 8. It might only have been a strong wind that turned hundreds of small forest fires into a single catastrophe. Once the great fires happened, the smoke became so thick it darked the skies and most navigation was brought to a halt for a few days. The *Detroit Free Press* told how shipping was stopped on Lake Huron as early as October 5 because of the dense smoke. The story said the atmosphere was blinding and the situation was the worst mariners could remember. The heavy smoke that dropped down over Lakes Michigan, Huron and Erie during October was blamed for a long string of wrecks, even as far east as Lake Ontario.

Many ships were put into service by their owners and their captains to help people along the shoreline escape the flames and later to bring medical and other services to them after the fires were over. The steamers *George L. Dunlap, Union* and *Favorite* were moored at Menomonee, Wisconsin, when the fire came. All three vessels carried hundreds of women and children from Menomonee and surrounding areas out into Lake Michigan while the men stayed behind to fight the fire. The *Dunlap* brought many survivors from the fire at Menomonee into Green Bay, Wisconsin on October 10.

The U. S. revenue cutter *Fesenden* was among the boats at work that week from Port Huron north into Michigan's Thumb District. This vessel put in at port after port, at first bringing medical attention to burn victims and surveying the extent of death and destruction. The *Fesenden* later carried supplies to the village of Port Austin, which was spared and consequently turned into a refugee center. Her first cargo to that community included ten barrels of flour, four barrels of pork, one barrel of sugar, one chest of tea, nine packages of clothing and a large quantity of crackers and cheese. Other cargo, shipped by the Detroit Relief Committee, was earmarked for distribution at other locations south of Port Austin, but the crew complained that the smoke was so dense they could not see to make a landing. After the *Fesenden* struck a rock, her captain decided to return to Port Huron with much of the cargo still aboard.

The steamer *Marine City*, which regularly stopped at Michigan coastal towns, saved many lives that week by car-

Schooner *Butcher Boy* was damaged in the Chicago fire, but later rebuilt.

rying people away as flames bore down on their homes. The steamer *Huron* brought hundreds of refugees to Port Huron on October 14 and then turned back to search for more.

While Chicago was the largest city destroyed by the fires, many other communities of lesser size also went up in flames. They included the town of Peshtigo, Wisconsin, where an estimated four hundred people perished, and surrounding settlements of Menekaunce, Sturgeon Bay, Menomonee and Birch Creek. Michigan communities lost included Holland, Manistee, Spring Lake, Grand Junction and Big Rapids in the western part of the lower peninsula, and Saginaw, Forestville, Craco, Tyre, White Rock, Huron City, Harbor Beach, Port Hope and Verona, all located in the eastern side along Lake Huron. Some of these towns were never rebuilt while others never were rebuilt to the size they originally were.

A report from Port Austin to the *Detroit Free Press* on October 13 said an estimated three thousand people were left homeless and many of them were suffering from burns in that area. "Hundreds are lying by the roadside, with no shelter and scarcely any clothing, and many of them severely burned," the story said.

Large areas of Wisconsin were burning on October 8. A report from Milwaukee to the *Detroit Free Press* said the lumber towns of Marinette and Peshtigo were lost. An untold number of people died. "The fires are now raging over three thousand square miles of territory. One hundred families have been burned out of their house and home and have taken refuge in Green Bay and other towns," the story said. "Houses, barns, farm buildings, bridges, fences and absolutely everything has been swept away and thousands of square miles of valuable forests destroyed. Bears and other wild beasts have been driven in disarray from the woods, and are fleeing in every direction across the fields."

James Manahan, a survivor of the Peshtigo fire, gave a first hand account to a reporter at Green Bay. He said the wind got so strong on the night of October 8 it was picking up large boards and causing them to tumble along. At 8:00 PM "we could hear the fire . . . roaring like the hum of a threshing machine. As the wind blew so strong, people were afraid it would reach the village, but nobody thought it would be what it was," Manahan said. "In less time than it takes to tell you, the houses on the west side of the river were all on fire, and the air was filled with showers of burning cinders."

Manahan said he and his wife fled their boarding house and started running to the river a few hundred feet away. "When we reached the road the air was filled with fire, and we had not left the house before it took fire. We hurried as fast as we could to the river and almost suffocated before we got there. Both sides of the river were in a blaze. We had to stay in the water from a little before ten o'clock until daylight the next morning. The heat was so great we had to keep our faces wet to prevent them from blistering. Our heads took fire and blazed up. Saw logs on the river took fire and fire seemed to be all around us. There was no chance to get away in any direction for the air was a mass of blaze."

When the fire was over, Manahan said the few survivors in the river found "not a house or fence or single board remained. Everything was swept off so it looked like a prairie. Even the railroad track was ruined, the ties being all burned up and the rails curled and crooked by the great heat." Bodies of humans and animals were scattered all over the ground. Before long, he said the stench rising from those bodies "was so powerful that we could not bear it."

Farther east, in Michigan's Huron County, the fire was bearing down on the little settlement of Rock Falls. Two families, the Manns and the Huxtables, escaped to a small fishing boat around 1:00 AM Monday morning. In the boat were the Huxtable family, Mr. Mann and five of his children. At first the families kept the boat tied up at the small dock and boat house because fierce westerly winds were blowing. Huxtable said they later were forced to cut the boat adrift when the fire spread to the boat house and threatened to burn their boat. He said they used a heavy stone to try to anchor the boat offshore, but the hurricane winds created by the fire drove them out into Lake Huron.

"At daybreak the smoke and ashes were so thick that we could not see the land nor the sun, and we could not determine our whereabouts," Huxtable said. The families were confined for about sixty hours in that small boat, without food. The children began to show the effects of their terrible ordeal

The *Favorite* was among the boats involved in rescue of survivors when fires swept the lake front communities.

on the second day. Everybody fled so quickly in the night the children had no time to get dressed. They spent the time on the water wearing only their bed clothes. Their only shelter was under the forward deck. Everybody was wet from the seas, which were continually splashing over the sides of the boat. Huxtable said it was not until sunrise on Wednesday morning that he saw enough light from the sun to determine east from west. At about that time, little Hermie Mann, age three, died in his father's arms. His last words were a request for food. The boat washed ashore near Kincardine, Ontario on the east side of Lake Huron, at about noon that same day.

As the fire approached the town of White Rock, a few miles south of Rock Falls, the people first formed a bucket brigade at the edge of town and attempted to fight it. When the wall of fire rolled out of the thick black smoke, it came at them with such fury everybody realized their cause was lost. They turned and fled for their lives into Lake Huron. All through that terrible night, men, women and children stood together in the water, watching their town burn. The air was so hot the people were forced to stay in the water for eight hours before anybody dared to get out. Wagons that had been partly driven into the water with personal belongings aboard were said to have caught fire and burned to the water line.

The steamer *Huron* stopped briefly on Monday. The ship was so filled with burn victims from other coastal towns that it didn't have room for the people at White Rock. It took on as many as could be squeezed aboard, and then steamed away into the smoke for Port Huron, leaving the rest behind.

Residents of the nearby lumber town of Cato were said to have saved their community. The men formed a bucket brigade at the mill and managed to dump sixty pails of water a minute on the buildings for an incredible fifty-six hours before the flames subsided.

Strangely enough, the fire didn't seem to hurt the lumber industry in Michigan. A report on the damage in the Saginaw Valley stated that less than twenty percent of the trees there were destroyed and that most lumber companies were still operating.

Strange Voyage of the *Moffat*

Port Huron, Mich.
Tuesday, October 10

Captain James Moffat put his tug, the *Frank Moffat,* at the disposal of the Port Huron Relief Committee. The tug left that port on Tuesday night with two large yawls in tow, each loaded with food, clothing and medical supplies.

The expedition steamed north, under the direction of Moffat and committee member Thomas Stevens. The smoke was so dense that the tug ran all night at slow speed, with the whistle sounding every few minutes. When dawn came, it was still impossible to see more than ten yards in any direction. The sailors coughed from inhaling the smoke. Every eye was red and sore.

Moffat, a veteran skipper on Lake Huron, was using every trick he knew to find his way. At 6:00 AM, when he thought he had traveled far enough, he changed course toward the Michigan shore, hoping to find Lexington or Forestville docks. The tug came upon the schooner *Sweepstakes,* lying at anchor with its sails reefed. The schooner crew said they had no idea where they were and had not seen land in four days. Birds, including a wild pigeon, came out of the smoke to land on the tug. The birds were exhausted and stayed aboard to rest, even though the men were only a few feet away, watching them.

At 7:00 AM land was spotted and a small boat sent ashore. The delegation landed at Purdy's place, five miles above White Rock. Purdy and three other families . . . 24 people in all . . . were staying together in an old shanty, twelve by sixteen feet. They said their homes had burned. These people wanted to stay and search for belongings and friends. They were given a barrel of crackers, bread, a ham and some tea.

From there the *Moffat* steamed south back to Forestville. There the sailors found utter desolation. "Not a house, barn or shed was left standing. Fruit trees are burned to black, leafless stubs. Hogs, cows, chickens and other animals are lying burned to a crisp where the flames overtook them. The huge mill chimney stands alone . . . a solitary monument, marking the site of what three days before was a thriving village of five hundred souls," said a story in the *Port Huron Weekly Times*. Both docks were burned, including all of the lumber and shingles stored there from the mill, awaiting shipment. People were beginning to arrive at the place from inland, having survived the fires. Provisions were left at Forestville before the *Moffat* steamed from there north to Sand Beach, the early name for what now is Harbor Beach.

When the boats arrived at that port they again found ruin and devastation. The *Weekly Times* story said that "all of the village, with the exception of Mr. Carrington's dwelling and store, is entirely consumed. Mill dock, dwellings, barns and other property, Robert Erwin's residence and store with stock of goods, Pritchley's hotel and others, are gone. The flames swept over the doomed village so swiftly that women and children escaped with nothing on but their night clothes."

The Carrington house had been opened as a shelter for survivors and the provisions from the store were exhausted by the time the *Moffat* arrived. Many of the people staying there were badly burned and in need of medical attention. About ten burn victims were loaded on the boats . . . some of them having to be carried suspended in a quilt . . . for the trip back to Port Huron. A Port Huron physician, identified as Dr.

Johnson, was aboard the *Moffat*. He dressed the burns and made the fire victims as comfortable as possible as they were brought aboard.

The boats went as far north as Forest Bay, taking on more burn victims and leaving supplies. Nearly every building at Forest Bay was burned, including John Hobson's mill and home. Because there was no firewood left north of Sand Beach for fueling the steamer, the *Moffat* was forced to turn south for Port Huron at 3:00 PM.

Dispatched Lumber Barges

Port Austin Reef
Off Saginaw Bay
Wednesday, Oct. 11

The tug *Dispatch* had five lumber laden barges, the *Paragon, Table Rock, Shiawassee, Shelden* and *Twilight* in tow when all six vessels went aground on Lake Huron's Port Austin Reef. Smoke may have been the cause.

A tug got busy and first pulled the barges off the reef. These boats were faithfully anchored offshore or lying in nearby harbors while salvagers turned their attention to the *Dispatch*, which was wedged hard on the rocks. Even the tug might have been salvaged but for the storm that hit the lakes on October 15. The blow destroyed the *Dispatch*.

It was such a bad storm that the waiting barge *Twilight* broke loose from its anchor and drifted off into Lake Huron with only the captain, mate and one other sailor aboard. The *Twilight* became waterlogged and its cabin washed away by the waves. The captain lashed everyone to the foremast and they remained there for twelve hours, exposed to the storm, until the schooner *Clayton Belle* rescued them the next day.

The *Twilight* drifted ashore at Kincardine, Ontario, with one hundred and thirty-four thousand feet of lumber aboard. The ship and cargo were later salvaged.

Wreck of the *Plover*

On Lake Superior
At Whitefish Point
Thursday, October 12

Smoke also may have been a factor in the wreck of the grain laden schooner *Plover* on the night of October 12. It was a narrow escape for Captain Jones and his crew of eight sailors when the *Plover* hit Whitefish Point and then bounded off into deep water to sink.

The crew came ashore in an open boat. Whitefish Point was uninhabited in 1871, much as it remains today so there was no shelter. To reach civilization the crew spent two days making its way in a small boat to Sault Ste. Marie. They arrived on Saturday, only hours before a killer storm struck.

There are no other details about the wreck of the *Plover*. The ship was sailing toward Sault Ste. Marie with eighteen thousand bushels of wheat in the hold when lost.

On the *Ella Doak*

On Lake Michigan
Saturday, October 14

The scow *Ella Doak* made its way across Lake Michigan in spite of heavy smoke. The boat's apparent owner, Captain John Doak, was returning home to a place called Williamsonville, Michigan, where he heard that the fire had destroyed his home and killed his wife and children. He was coming home to mourn.

Doak went ashore to attend the task of burying the dead. He sent the ship back to Milwaukee with a three-member crew aboard. The time frame of these events is not clear. During the trip back to Milwaukee, the first mate, named Congor, crushed his hand in a shipboard accident. Then a serious gale developed and the two able seamen, Charles King and Charles McGehan, were left with the job of bringing the vessel through the storm on their own.

They did it. The *Doak* arrived at Milwaukee with one mast and much of its canvass wrecked. The ship's wheel also was smashed by the tempest. The fact that King and McGehan brought the vessel into port safely was noted in several area newspapers.

Death Gale

On Lake Michigan
Saturday, October 14

Even before the smoke from the fires cleared, a mighty storm swept the lakes to cause even more death and destruction. The gale began on Saturday night on Lake Michigan and within hours spread east across Lakes Huron and Erie. Sailors said the storm came on them like a hurricane.

Its first victim was the schooner *Levant*, under command of Captain Patrick Lyons, which capsized off Sheboygan, Wisconsin. The boat later drifted ashore to be pounded into a pile of rubble.

The story of the *Levant* was told to the *Detroit Tribune* by Peter J. Thornum, the only survivor. Thornum said the ship, loaded with lumber, had been running all day before a stiff breeze from the south southwest. That night the wind increased to a gale. When a squall hit at about 9:00 PM, the schooner went over on its beam ends somewhere between Sheboygan and Port Washington.

Thornum said he and the other sailors on the deck felt the ship going over and everybody ran for the side. The *Levant* didn't go all the way over, but stayed on its side. The men lashed themselves to the rigging to keep from being carried away by the waves sweeping over them. The water was very cold and the sailors suffered from exposure. At about 11:00 PM the lights of a passing ship were seen. The vessel came within a hundred and fifty feet of the wreck and the men yelled at the top of their lungs. They failed to make themselves heard against the sound of the gale. No other vessels were seen that night. When daylight came, only Thornum, and sailors Peter Brant and a man known only as Charlie remained alive. Captain Lyons and First Mate Robert Brown were dead, as well as sailors Bill Smith, William Shills and the steward, a German named Kloss. All had fallen away into the sea where their bodies floated, still tied to the ship's ropes.

The schooner *D. P. Dobbins* came upon the wreck a few hours after daylight. The *Dobbins'* mate, John Bolin, commanded the life boat that came up to the wreck. He tossed a line and Thornum grabbed it. Thornum said he knew Charlie and Brant were both senseless and unable to help themselves. He could reach Charlie so he tied the rope around the man's chest and signaled Bolin to pull him aboard. "But he got tangled in the rigging and drowned before our eyes," he said.

After that, Thornum managed to get the rope off Charlie's body and tie it around himself. Bolin pulled him into the life boat. The problem then was getting Brant into the boat. "He was out of his head and he just hung there and stared at us with set and glassy eyes," Thornum said. "Bolin finally made a lasso and threw it over his head and hauled him into the boat. But he was so far gone he died about ten or fifteen minutes later."

Gilbert Demont's Last Command

On Lake Huron
Sunday, October 15

Capt. Gilbert Demont's only mark on history: he is remembered as the master of the ill-fated propeller *R. G. Coburn* who went down with his ship on stormy Lake Huron.

Beer's *History of the Great Lakes* paints a romantic picture of Demont, standing just aft of the texas with his hand on the rail as the *Coburn* made its final plunge. Survivors accounts and government documents suggest, however, that Demont's image as a hero may not have been deserved. There is evidence that he was an incompetent and inexperienced mariner who foolishly got his ship caught in the middle of a killer storm and then didn't know what to do.

The record shows that Demont temporarily replaced a retiring master a few days earlier and was scheduled to turn over the command to Capt. John Condon, of Buffalo, in a few days. Condon, in fact, was a passenger on the *Coburn* when it sank somewhere off Harbor Beach, Michigan, taking sixteen passengers and fifteen members of the ship's crew to the bottom with it. Condon was a survivor.

Peter J. Ralph, Eighth District Supervising Inspector of Steamships, suggested in his report that Demont was negligent in the way he handled the ship. "If the anchors had been let go, so as to have brought the vessel's head to the wind, as the depth of the water in the locality of the disaster is only from thirty to forty fathoms, and the vessel having good anchors, with ninety fathoms of chain each, there is a probability that this loss of life and property might have been lessened, if not entirely avoided," Ralph wrote.

Ralph also reported that the *Coburn* was properly equipped with life boats, and that he believed everybody aboard the ship could have escaped the sinking if the lifeboats had been properly managed. "Two metallic life boats were picked up on the Canada shore, right side up, which evidently were not used, except by two of the crew, Porter and Barber, who were found dead on the beach near where the boats came ashore. The eighteen survivors had the wooden boats," Ralph noted.

Historians have attempted to link the disaster to the great forest fire. It is true that the smoke from the fire was still hanging over the lakes when the *Coburn* started its fatal trip from Duluth to Buffalo. Second Mate W. L. Hanes, a survivor, said Demont was concerned about the poor visibility and chose after nightfall to keep the steamer's engines in check and the ship virtually parked in one spot in the middle of Lake Huron. Had the boat been traveling at good speed, it might have slipped past the open and deadly waters of Saginaw Bay and escaped the brunt of the southwest gale that claimed her.

The *Coburn* was carrying about seventy people and a cargo of wheat, flour and barrels of silver ore. It followed the steamer *Empire* most of the day until the *Empire* stopped at Presque Isle on Saturday evening. John Gray, of Marquette, Michigan, who claimed to have been a passenger, said the gale was developing when the *Coburn* passed Presque Isle.

The *R. G. Coburn* sank in Lake Huron during an October storm.

Gray said that while other vessels were running for shelter with all speed, Demont foolishly ordered the *Coburn* to steam dead ahead into the storm.

Mate Hanes rebutted Gray's charge. He said the weather was fair and Demont had no thought of putting in when the ship passed Presque Isle harbor. He said that by 10:00 PM, however, the wind was blowing fresh from the northeast and the ship was rolling heavily. Hanes said there was so much smoke in the air that Demont turned the ship's bow into the wind and checked down the engines. By turning the boat so the hull was taking the seas head on, he made conditions as comfortable as possible for the passengers. His plan was to wait until morning when visibility improved.

Demont did not expect the storm that struck the ship out of the southwest a few hours later. As the seas grew, the boat began rolling and passengers became alarmed. Everybody was awake and dressed by 3:00 AM when the storm reached its peak. Passengers were seasick. Hanes said the boat held its own until about 4:00 AM when, somewhere off Thunder Bay, the rudder was lost. Hanes said he was standing watch in the wheelhouse when the rudder failed. "On working the wheel it revolved so easily that it was at once evident that something was wrong with the steering gear. At first it was supposed that the chains had parted, but an investigation soon showed that the rudder was gone."

After the rudder was lost, the *Coburn* broached so that the seas hit her broadside. The ship began coming apart. The smoke stack fell and smashed the cabin area. On the main deck, barrels of flour and silver ore broke loose and smashed holes in the bulwarks. The ship took on water.

Hanes said the cargo shifted to leeward and it became impossible to keep the ship trimmed. Workers cut holes in the bulwarks and worked through the night, tossing cargo overboard, hoping to save the *Coburn*. The final blow came at about dawn while the ship lay heeled over to port at an awkward angle. A powerful wave rolled over the decks and smashed open the fireman's gangway. Cascades of water now rushed into the ship's exposed hold with every angry sea, and it was only going to be minutes before the *Coburn* sank. As the ship settled, Hanes said the crew made a frantic effort to launch life boats. Demont sent word to the passengers "to prepare for the worst. But very few left their cabins. Most were sick and they did not care to make the effort to save themselves."

Hanes said the two yawl boats were launched. He said he took seven people with him in one and ten others got in the second yawl boat just as the *Coburn* sank stern first from under their feet. The boats floated off the deck. The mate said he didn't think any other boats got away.

Captain Condon said he saw a third boat get away before the *Coburn* went down. He said he shared a boat with Thomas Derrin, John Bridgman, Spencer Churchwell, Henry Munford and John Young. A second boat got away with about nine people aboard, and the third boat had about fifteen people in it. "A fourth boat was on the davits, filled with people, and was being launched when the *Coburn* gave a heavy lurch and immediately sank out of sight. The small boat filled with people was swamped, and we afterwards saw them in the water," Condon said.

"When the *Coburn* went down, her upper cabin was burst off and we afterwards saw it floating away, covered with people. Before the *Coburn* went down, I saw Captain Demont standing on the starboard arch, when a large wave struck him and threw him in the lake. When he rose he caught a barrel that was floating near him, but he soon sank again and disappeared," Condon said.

Condon's boat was picked up by the bark *Robert Gaskin* at about 4:00 PM. By then the storm was abating and the seas were diminished enough that the rescue was not difficult. Eight other survivors, including Hanes, were picked up by the bark *Zack Chandler* about thirty miles off Pointe aux Barques at about the same time. The survivors were taken to Mackinaw.

The third lifeboat described by Condon apparently capsized. Two boats drifted ashore at Kincaradine, Ontario. One of them was empty and two bodies were found either in or near the other boat. Bodies, barrels of flour and wreckage drifted ashore along the Canadian coast for many days.

Other survivors included H. M. Rhodes, Martin Maharring, James Warwick, F. Mumford, Charles Miller, James Ludner, James McQueen and R. Kelley. These were a mixture of passengers and crew. None of the women and children aboard the ship survived. The dead included first mate William W. Simmons of Detroit, first engineer A. S. Robinson of Marine City, second engineer Frank Hutchinson of Detroit, steward George S. Westcott and his wife of Marine City, clerk Edward Major of Fromfield, Ontario, porter Charles Mignault of Detroit, and passengers Mrs. Thomas Holton and Mary Maun of Cincinatti, and Helen Palmer of Toledo.

McQueen, one of the men in the boat picked up by the *Chandler,* said he woke up at about 4:00 AM to find the ship rocking violently. The storm got steadily worse. When he went out on deck at about 6:00 o'clock, McQueen said he knew the ship was in serious trouble. By then, he said the smoke stack had toppled and he could hear freight barrels tumbling about on the main deck. When Simmons ordered all hands below to lighten the load, McQueen said he and several other passengers joined the workers in the task. He said he returned to the open deck just moments before the ship sank. He said he found a life boat and got in it before it was pitched out into the water. The *Coburn* sank with a cargo of fifteen thousand bushels of wheat, thirty-five hundred barrels of flour and thirty barrels of silver ore. It was said that the wreck lies in twenty-one fathoms of water, about six and one-half miles off Harbor Beach. To date, the wreck has not been found.

It had been a troublesome year for the *Coburn.* The propeller hit a rock while steaming in dense fog off Keewenaw

The propellers *R. G. Coburn,* at left, and *Norman,* docked side by side at Duluth in 1871.

Point on Lake Superior on June 6, and put a large hole in the bottom. The crew ran the ship into shallow water in the north entrance to Portage Lake Canal before the boat sank. A cargo of two hundred and fifty barrels of flour and supplies for local traders had to be thrown overboard.

The *Coburn* broke its crank pin and stranded on Lake Superior in September. At the time of that accident, the steamer was coming down from Duluth to Erie, Pennsylvania with a load of wheat and flour and the schooner *St. Paul* in tow. The *St. Paul* put up sails and towed the *Coburn* back to Duluth.

The *Coburn* was built for the Ward Line the year before at Marine City. It measured one hundred and ninety-three feet in length.

Lone Survivor

On Lake Huron
Sunday, October 15

The same storm that sank the *Coburn* wrecked the three masted schooner *Excelsior* somewhere off Thunder Bay. Crew member Charles Lostrom of Erie, Pennsylvania, was the only survivor.

Lostrom's chilling story can be found on the pages of his hometown newspaper, the *Erie Observer,* stored on microfilm in the Erie Public Library. Lostrom told how he survived the wreck, then spent fifty-eight hours clinging to a piece of floating wreckage before he was rescued by fishermen at Southhampton, Ontario. He was blown about a hundred and twenty-five miles from where the *Excelsior* went down.

The ship was apparently coming around the lakes from Chicago, bound for Buffalo. Lostrom said the vessel had "a rapid run past the Manitous and through the straits to False Presque Isle, on Lake Huron, with a fair wind all the way. At False Presque Isle we could not lay our course. It was blowing fresh and we ran in and anchored Tuesday afternoon (Oct. 10). We laid there until Wednesday noon, when we got under way and stood out into the lake. Finding the sea heavy and the wind ahead, we ran back and anchored in seven fathoms of water, half way between Middle Island and Thunder Bay light, as we supposed."

Lostrom said the crew could only guess at their location because the smoke from the forest fires was so thick that for a few days nobody could see land to get a bearing. While anchored, he said a steam barge came upon them and the boat's captain was lost in the smoke. He asked the *Excelsior's* master, Capt. Samuel Gintz, where he was. Gintz could only give an approximate location.

The weather cleared later in the week, and Gintz ordered the sails set once again. The schooner was beating down past Thunder Bay when the big storm struck from the south southwest early on Sunday morning. Lostrom said he was at the wheel until 2:00 AM and that he knew the ship was laboring. "The pumps were constantly tried, all (crew members) were very anxious, and (everybody) stayed on deck from midnight until the vessel was wrecked" at about 4:30 AM. Lostrom said the gale carried away the main sail and later the halyards. After that it was almost impossible to control the ship.

The crew set all of the square sails they could and attempted to keep the schooner running before the wind. Gintz knew his ship was sinking. It had been taking on water for several hours. "After making the sails and when all hands were at the pumps, Captain Gintz went around to all the men and shook hands with every one, saying 'Good bye, boys, we are going.'" Lostrom said nobody wanted to believe him at first. He said he went out on the deck with Gintz to help cut away the boat tackle falls, but they were too late. The *Excelsior* was swept by a large wave and foundered under their feet.

Lostrom said he was drawn deep in the water with the sinking ship. When he thought he could not hold his breath another moment he broke to the surface. There he discovered that he was alone. He called out but nobody answered. He said he swam to a piece of the cabin roof, about fourteen by sixteen feet square, and got on it. "I looked around and saw some distance off, and out of hail of me, four of the crew clinging to what was apparently a plank. I saw them and they saw me, but they soon disappeared from me.

"There were things floating around me . . . pieces of the cabin and some provisions. The only thing I could get hold of was some apples that floated near me. I put them in my pockets. The piece of the cabin roof that I was on was broken in two, crosswise about the middle of it; the mizzen mast went through it, and it broke off right in the middle of the hole the mast went through. Two of the planks on the roof, one on each side of the hole, projected outward. I sat in that hole on the cabin roof, holding on to the projecting broken off planks on each side of me, with my arms resting on it and my legs and feet hanging down in the water.

"I was pretty warmly clothed with woolen clothes and stockings and thick boots, and over all my clothes I had an oil coat and oil pants and a southwester on my head. To this I probably owe my life for the oil clothes were air tight. The sea would run all over my frail support making it very difficult for me to hold my place, and I was washed off repeatedly."

Lostrom remained on this makeshift raft for two days and two nights before he was rescued. "All day Sunday and Sunday night the wind blew a fierce gale and a heavy sea was running. It required the use of all my senses and strength to carry me through the awful long night." He said the storm abated on Monday. After the raft stopped rolling, Lostrom said he discovered that he could stand up, which was a great relief because his feet were swollen.

"I found a piece of board and used it for a paddle to work my way before the wind, though I did not know which way I was going. I tore up a piece of canvass covering the cabin roof and put my board against it and set my back against that. It made a very good sail and helped me along some. All day Monday I was floating along in this way." For some reason, Lostrom said he preferred to remain on his feet. He said he remained standing until he was taken off the raft on Tuesday morning.

"After dark Monday night I saw a light, which afterwards proved to be South Hampton light on the Canada side of Lake Huron and at the mouth of Sagren River. During Monday night my mind began to wander, and I began to lose my senses. I was aware of it, and by great effort once in a while could arouse myself. I seemed to be in a sort of dreamy stupor. All that long Monday night, my second night on my frail support, I stood upon my feet and watched and waited for the coming of the next morning. I did not suffer from a sense of hunger, but I suffered a good deal from cold. I could see the light all night at South Hampton.

"Tuesday morning after daylight, some fishing boats put out from South Hampton to lift their nets. There were several of them. I was seven or eight miles out in the lake. They saw me, but supposed I was a buoy or a root of a floating tree. I saw them plainly enough but I stood up there so unconscious that I did not know enough to make any signs to them. I was in a sort of dream."

It was late in the afternoon when fisherman Allan McDonald thought he noticed movement in the strange floating object he had been watching nearby. McDonald brought his boat closer to have a look. He and sailors John Graham and George MacAulay were surprised to discover that the thing they had been watching was a living man, standing on a piece of floating wreckage.

The *Excelsior* was built in Buffalo in 1865. It originally was rigged as a bark, but had been converted as a schooner during the winter of 1870-71. The boat measured one hundred and fifty-six feet in length.

Saving the *R. P. Mason*

Northern Lake Michigan
Off Cross Village, Mich.
Sunday, October 15

The schooner *R. P. Mason* had been aground at Waugoshance Point in the Straits of Mackinaw since October 8 and the tug *Leviathan* was working there, trying to get the vessel free.

Success came on Saturday, only hours before the storm hit. The stricken *Mason* had a large hole in the hull, which was temporarily patched with canvass. Two heavy steam powered pumps were hoisted to the deck and fired to keep the ship afloat while the tug pulled it toward the safely of Little Traverse Bay. The two boats sailed right into the heart of the same gale that sank the *Coburn* and *Excelsior*.

The schooner *R. P. Mason* killed several members of a salvage crew when it capsized in a storm on Lake Michigan

The *Mason* was lost again. One story said the tow line separated from the strain and part of it got caught in one of the *Leviathan's* propellers, making it difficult for the tug to maneuver. Another version said the tow line got tangled in the propeller while the *Mason* was under tow, and the crew of the *Leviathan* was forced to cut the line. The schooner broached, rolled on its beam ends, and dumped the two overheated steam pumps from her deck. Capt. Thomas Phall, three sailors and the steam pump engineer were drowned. The other victims were identified as E. Martin, Louis Hale, William Beeba and a man named Hanson. Four workers held onto the overturned hull until they were rescued by a small boat from shore.

The *Mason* drifted ashore upside down near Cross Village and remained there a derelict. Some said it was a total loss. But the boat wasn't finished yet. It was salvaged and put back in service the next year.

A cargo of nine thousand bushels of corn and oats, one hundred and fifty barrels of pork, fifty barrels of beef, a hundred and twenty-five barrels of flour and other sundries had been partly removed by the *Leviathan* and taken to Milwaukee the week before.

The *Mason* had a relatively long life on the lakes after that. It was converted into a barge in 1905, and served until 1917 when a fire claimed it on Lake Michigan. It was not a large vessel. It measured one hundred and sixteen feet in length. It was built in 1867 at Ferrysburg, Michigan.

Capsizing of *La Petite*

On Lake Huron
Sunday, Oct. 15

The storm caught the schooner *La Petite* at about 4:00 AM. The boat, with Capt. O. B. Smith at the helm, was sailing from Alpena to Huron, Ohio, with a load of lumber. The crew said the gale came on them like a tornado, driving the ship off its course. Heavy green-gray seas began rolling over the decks. The force of the water overcame the rope stays and within a short time swept away the boat's deck load.

The schooner *La Petite* capsized in a Lake Huron storm. It was salvaged and remained on the lakes another thirty-two years.

As the storm intensified, the *La Petite* took on water, waterlogged, and then capsized. Smith and his wife, who was working as ship's cook, and four other sailors scrambled over the rail as the ship rolled on its side. The schooner *E. P. Dorr*, under command of a Captain Barns, came on them at dusk. Everybody was still alive, clinging to the floating wreck but suffering from the cold lake water and exhaustion. The *Dorr* took them to Au Sable.

The wreck was found by the tug *Brockway* off Southhampton, Ontario, and towed to Port Huron. The *La Petite* was lengthened the following year from ninety-five to one hundred and nineteen feet. It continued sailing the lakes until 1903, when the boat stranded at Clay Banks, Wisconsin. It was built at Huron, Ohio, in 1866.

Escaping Disaster

Northern Lake Huron
Off Detour, Michigan
Sunday, October 15

The schooner *Morning Light* was yet another victim of the October blow. It was carrying a load of iron ore from Superior when caught by the storm early Sunday. Violent squalls followed by a storm out of the southwest carried away the foreboom and gaft and fouled the main sail so it could not be taken in. To save the ship from almost certain disaster, the crew jettisoned the deck load of ore, then ran before the wind to Detour. As the vessel approached the shore, the anchors were dropped in the hope of keeping the ship from destroying itself on the rocky shore. The anchors slowed down the boat's headlong rush to disaster, but just barely. One of the chains parted and the other anchor slipped so the *Morning Light* drifted ashore anyway. It landed softly. Tugs pulled the boat off intact the next day.

Other Gale Hardships

The storm of October 15 wrecked and damaged a fleet of other vessels. Any record of their fate was nearly lost in the volumes of news reports that flowed during that hectic week. Their brief stories follow:

➥The schooner *H. C. Winslow* capsized in the gale Sunday night off Point Becile, Lake Michigan. Three women passengers were trapped below deck and drowned. The crew escaped.

➥The bark *Masilon* rammed the north pier while entering the Sault Ste Marie locks and sank in the channel. The wreck blocked shipping for several hours until it was pumped out and towed away.

➥The schooner *Lucinda Van Valkenburg* went ashore with a cargo of grain at Presque Isle on Lake Huron. The propeller *City of New York* pulled her off after the crew jettisoned five thousand bushels of wheat.

➥The new three-masted schooner *John Burt* was anchored at Leland on Lake Michigan, waiting to unload coal, when the storm hit. The *Burt* dragged its anchors and went into shoal water. The crew flooded the ship to keep it from pounding to pieces. A series of bad storms after that delayed salvage, and by November 1 the *Burt* was declared a total wreck. It was said the hull was so badly hogged and strained it wasn't worth saving.

➥The schooner *Northern Belle* was caught in the gale on Lake Michigan. It was bound for Chicago with coal. The boat shipped its rudder, dropped its centerboard and split its sails. The crew anchored off Point Betsey and waited for the storm to abate, then came ashore on a raft. Nearly half of the cargo was jettisoned. The ship later was towed by a tug to Manistee, Mich.

➥The schooner *George J. Whitney,* laden with coal, ran on Sugar Island Reef at exactly the same place the propeller *Tweed* hit nearly two weeks earlier. The ship was abandoned on October 25 after three steam pumps failed to get the water out of the hold. The *Whitney* was salvaged the next spring.

➥The propeller *Empire* went aground at Pointe aux Barques, Lake Huron, and later was pulled free.

➥The schooner *Clayton Belle,* loaded with grain, went ashore at Presque Isle Point. The crew threw thirty-five hundred bushels of wheat overboard before the boat worked free.

➥Schooners *Imperial* and *Eleanor* collided on Lake Huron. Neither ship was sunk, but both were damaged and brought into dry dock for repair. The *Imperial* earlier went ashore at False Presque Isle and didn't get free until a hundred tons of iron ore were tossed overboard.

➥The propeller *Galena* went aground on Tawas Point. The steamer *Eighth Ohio* removed passengers and a large number of horses. The ship was pulled off three days later by the tug *Vulcan.*

➥The schooner *John S. Miner* went ashore near Kincardine, Ontario and broke up. It was a total loss.

➥The schooner *David Ferguson* drifted ashore near Kincardine, Ontario, when blown off course from Duluth to Buffalo. The crew was saved. The *Ferguson* later was raised and towed to Detroit, her deck badly hogged and the hull severely damaged.

➥The propeller *Japan* became unmanageable on the Detroit River during the storm and went aground at the lower end of Fighting Island. The boat was pulled free the next day.

➥The schooner *Victoria,* loaded with wheat, was bound from Detroit to Oswego, New York when it went ashore in dense smoke on Ford's Shoals on Lake Ontario a few hours before the storm hit. The crew came ashore in a yawl boat. The *Victoria* pounded to pieces in the storm.

Visiting Michigan Fire Victims

Southern Lake Huron
Along the Michigan coast
Sunday, October 15

The storm delayed the work of a relief committee which was attempting to bring supplies from Port Huron north to the people along the fire ravaged shores of Lake Huron.

The government revenue ship *Fessenden,* under command of Captain Fitzgerald, got under way late Sunday after the worst of the gale abated. It steamed from Port Huron with key members of the committee aboard. Once the steamer began rolling on the open waters of Lake Huron, everybody held on and did their best not to become seasick.

A writer for the *Detroit Daily Post* was among the passengers. He said in a story published on October 18 that the wind had blown much of the smoke away "so that the land and its cheerless forests, bared of leaves, black and gaunt with the charred pines, stood boldly out as we passed."

The decks of the *Fessenden* were piled high with supplies which included barrels of flour, pork, cheese, apples, bread, bundles of clothing, blankets and bedding, boots and shoes. The supplies were piled on the open deck because the ship was never designed to carry freight.

The steamer made its first stop at White Rock, where the people made a make-shift walkway out to a partially standing pier. Workers carried supplies ashore there. The committee found about two hundred people living in the two houses and the one barn spared by the fire. The rest of the community was in ashes. The survivors said that the town of Paris, several miles inland, was leveled. People there were said to be living in a school and others in holes dug in the ground.

The next stop was at Rock Falls, where the survivors had battled for three days to save their town. About two hundred people were found there. Farther north, the *Fessenden* encountered smoke and was forced to drop anchor for the night. A small boat was sent ashore the next day and it was learned that the ship was anchored a mile off Port Hope. A tannery, Stafford's Mill, a warehouse, the pier and five or six homes were burned, but the rest of Port Hope, a town of about three hundred and fifty people, was still standing.

The next town on the peninsula, Huron City, was found to have been destroyed. Only one house remained. People there told how two men attempted to escape the fire in an open boat and were blown out to sea. They were presumed dead.

Capsized on Lake Ontario

Off Oswego, New York
Wednesday, October 18

Remnants of the gale were still causing trouble on Lake Ontario as the schooner *Olivia,* under command of Captain Bradbeer, set sail from Mill Point to Oswego. The ship rolled so badly that the cook, John Dewey, became seasick and collapsed in his bunk below deck. It cost him his life. When the *Olivia* capsized at about 10:00 AM, Dewey was trapped there to drown.

All other crew members were apparently on deck and survived. The sailors hung to the sides of the overturned ship for about an hour before someone cut the yawl loose. They climbed aboard, huddling there in the cold, wet day, until the boat drifted ashore seven miles from Oswego.

The Revenue Cutter *Chase* found the wreck the following Monday, October 23, and towed it into Sackett's Harbor. Dewey's body was not found.

Loss of the *Eliza Logan*

On Lake Erie
Near Erie, Pa.
Thursday, October 19

Captain Lawson and one sailor drowned when the schooner *Eliza Logan* foundered in rough weather on Lake Erie, about twelve miles from Erie.

The *Logan* was bound from Toledo to Buffalo with a load of wheat when it went down at about noon. Six crew members scrambled into the ship's crosstrees and were still there when the schooner *Emu* found them at 6:00 AM Saturday. It was said the survivors hung by their hands from the crosstrees on the main mast for forty-two hours. The *Emu* took them to Port Colborne.

The schooner Eliza Logan foundered in Lake Erie in 1871.

Shooting at His Burning Tug

Lakeport, Michigan
Friday, October 27

There was a strange story in the November 2 edition of the *Port Huron Weekly Times* about a Captain King, who stood at the dock at Lakeport firing shots from his pistol into the hull of his burning tugboat, *Eclipse*.

The incident happened October 27 while the tug was tied up to take on wood for fuel. Workers on the tug *Goodnow*, who apparently stopped at Port Huron on their way to Detroit, told how King was recklessly firing his weapon even before the fire broke out. One slug struck a man aboard the *Eclipse*. The story did not explain how seriously injured the victim was or give a name.

When the fire was discovered, the story said the tug was pushed away from the dock with a ladder, used like a pole. Then King "bid her adieu" by emptying the contents of his pistol into the burning ship. The story did not explain King's irrational behavior, nor did it say whether he was arrested for shooting anybody.

A November 4 story in the *Manistee Times* told of the burning, but did not mention anything abnormal about the actions of the captain. It said the fire started in the boiler room. The *Eclipse* was docked in shallow water so efforts to scuttle it to save the hull were unsuccessful, the story said.

Fire on Mud Lake

On Munuscong Lake
Sunday, October 29

The propeller *Dean Richmond* was snaking its way through unfamiliar territory when it dropped anchor on Munuscong Lake, commonly called "Mud Lake," to wait out the night under a heavy bank of smoke. Instead of following its usual route between Buffalo and Chicago, the *Richmond's* owners had sent the steamer on a special trip into Lake Superior. Because they were not familiar with the winding, twisting route from the St. Marys River through the islands into Lake Huron, and because visibility in the smoke-filled air was poor, Capt. James Pratt chose to drop a hook and wait out the night about a mile above Round Island.

The ship was still there when fire broke out in a pantry and spread to the promenade deck at 5:30 AM. Discovery was hampered by an already smoke filled atmosphere so the blaze gained much headway before the crew realized the boat was burning. The blaze was soon threatening the lives of the forty-two passengers and crew members.

There were conflicting stories about what happened. One account said the chief engineer tried to attach a fire hose to a pony engine, but the smoke drove him out of the engine room before he got the fire hoses charged. Another story said the crew attempted to charge the fire hoses, but that equipment on the eight-year-old boat was in such poor repair, nothing worked. Thus it was that the fire was skipping out of control across the painted wooden decks. Boats were lowered but the fire was so threatening many people didn't wait and jumped overboard. Gang planks, fenders and loose pieces of wood were thrown into the water for survivors to hang onto until help came.

The *Dean Richmond* was extensively damaged and sunk by a fire on Mud Lake.

The *Detroit Tribune* accused Captain Pratt and six other members of the crew of dereliction of duty. The story said Pratt and the others were the first to leave the ship in one of the life boats. There were reports of pandemonium aboard the burning vessel as passengers were left behind to fend for themselves. Pratt later was blamed for the death of the ship's chambermaid, identified in one account as Mona Botsford, and in another as Lucy Mora. Witnesses said the woman drowned after she lost her grip on a piece of wood she was sharing with First Mate James Edgecomb. Everybody else was pulled into the life boats. The boats landed at Round Island and were picked up the next day by the passing steamer *Mineral Rock.*

The *Richmond* was extensively damaged by the fire before it settled to the bottom of the shallow lake. A cargo of wheat was lost. Salvagers later raised the wreck and towed it to Buffalo where it was rebuilt in 1873 at a cost of one hundred and thirty-five thousand dollars. The *Dean Richmond* continued to work the lakes for another twenty years before sinking with all hands on Lake Erie in 1893. The *Richmond* was built at Buffalo in 1864. It held the distinction of being one of the largest vessels on the lakes in its day, measuring two hundred and thirty-eight feet in length. It had a cargo capacity of over a thousand gross tons.

The Strange Disappearance of Captain McDonald

At Buffalo, New York
Saturday, October 28

Captain John McDonald wasn't acting right. The crew said he was pacing the quarter deck aboard his command, the Canadian barge *Hotchkiss,* that Friday morning in an obvious distressed state of mind. He told fellow officers that he couldn't sleep and that he thought something was wrong with him.

McDonald seemed to calm down that afternoon and by evening things appeared to be back to normal. Or were they? That was the last anybody ever saw of McDonald. When the mate looked in on him Saturday morning, McDonald was gone. A blood stained knife and large pool of blood were found on the cabin floor. From there, a trail of blood led up a ladder to the deck and then to the rail.

It appeared that Captain McDonald was dead even though his body was not found. Was it a murder? Did someone kill McDonald and then throw his body overboard? Or did McDonald stab himself . . . then drag himself to the rail and throw himself into the water to drown? Because of his state of mind the previous day, and because the knife was found on the floor, authorities opted for the suicide story. Nobody really knew.

The Ship That Wrecked The Train

Chicago, Illinois
Wednesday, November 1

Captain Duane Rider and Chief Engineer Morris Shay were arrested and jailed on charges of wrecking a moving train with their ship, the tug *George B. McClellan.* The arrest followed one of the strangest accidents in Chicago history. It happened about a month after the city was leveled by fire.

Rider and Shay were charged with driving the tug into the side of a Northwestern Railway pivoting bridge over the Chicago River when an eight car passenger train was approaching it. The impact caused the bridge to swing open as the train, operated by Engineer Ed Pierce and fireman Charles Hall was only a few feet away.

Hall jumped to safety but Engineer Pierce stayed to try to stop the train and save the passengers in the cars behind him. He and a railroad clerk, William Lee, who was hitching a ride in the cab, rode the engine and tender into the river. The rest of the train did stop and the coupler connecting the tender to the baggage car parted, so no other cars took the plunge. Lee was killed but Pierce lived. Witnesses pulled him from the water. He was hospitalized with serious injuries.

Rider said the bridge normally swung open for his tug when he approached. This day, while bringing the tug toward the bridge at about 4:00 PM, he gave a blast on the whistle to let the bridge tender know he was coming. He said he noticed the train approaching and signaled Engineer Shay to reduce speed. He said he planned to let the boat drift toward the bridge. Either Shay failed to slow the tug or Rider miscalculated its speed. When he saw the boat was going to hit the bridge, Rider said he sent another signal, ordering Shay to reverse the engines. The signal came too late. The bow of the tug hit the bridge hard enough to jar it open.

The tug *George B. McClellan* may have been the only Great Lakes boat to have caused a train wreck.

GALES OF NOVEMBER

For Lack of a Tug

Off Cleveland Harbor
On Lake Erie
Wednesday, November 1

The scow *American Eagle* arrived at Cleveland with a load of limestone from Marblehead at about 10:00 PM Tuesday. The scow beat back and forth just outside the breakwater, waiting for a tug to escort it into the harbor. When no tug appeared, the captain dropped anchor and planned to wait until morning before coming in under sail.

It seemed to be the right thing to do. The lake was smooth that night with a moderate south breeze blowing. Things changed within hours. Sometime after midnight the wind veered around to the northwest and began building. By 5:00 AM a full force gale was in the making. The captain decided to weigh anchor and make a run for the harbor. The crew drew up the hook, but before they got sails set, the scow drifted into the west pier. It struck with a sickening jolt which smashed the stern. The wreck then drifted into some nearby rocks.

The crew escaped to shore in a lifeboat, but the *American Eagle* broke up and was a total loss.

Wreck of the *Courtright*

On Lake Michigan
Off Racine, Wisconsin
Tuesday, November 7

When the schooner *M. Courtright* became waterlogged in rough weather, Captain William Durgan dropped the anchor off Racine and tried to wait for a calmer sea. The anchor dragged and the *Courtright* drifted on the rocks, about a mile south of the harbor, and pounded to a total wreck. The crew escaped.

The United States revenue cutter *Andrew Johnson* steamed into the harbor that week. When the *Johnson* returned to Milwaukee on November 11 the crew reported that the ship could not be saved. They meant what they said when they reported the boat a wreck.

The *Courtright's* mainmast, rail, stanchions, bulwarks and stern were gone, the deck was broken up, and the hull split in two both fore and aft. The beach was strewn with lumber from the wreck for miles in both directions. One anchor was still down, but the other was still in its place at the rail. Would things have been different if Durgan had dropped both anchors?

The *Courtright* was built in 1856.

Trouble With Rocks

On Lake George
Tuesday, November 7

The new iron steamer *India* was among the first lakers built with compartments so Captain Ben Wilkins believed, as other sailors did in 1871, that the ship was almost unsinkable. That probably explained why he didn't pause after the steamer hit a rock in the Sault Ste Marie canal. He ordered the boat backed off the obstacle, then continued down the river into Lake George.

The propeller *India* sank after it struck a rock in the St. Marys River.

It was on Lake George that the *India* had the misfortune of striking a second rock. This time there was no way for Wilkins to ignore the damage. His crew reported serious flooding. Wilkins learned to his horror that the ship's compartments were not as water tight as he had believed and that the ship was sinking.

Lake George is a small body of water and Wilkins had time to run the *India* aground before it settled to the bottom. The boat remained there four or five days before the tug *Wilcox* arrived from Detroit with salvage equipment and steam pumps. The *Wilcox* got the *India* refloated, then towed it to Buffalo. On the way, the steam pumps tossed great streams of water over the sides of the ship. The pumps kept the *India* afloat until the partially damaged cargo of wheat and barrels of flour were unloaded and the ship pulled into dry dock for repair.

The *India* served a long seventy-seven-year career. The vessel was scrapped in 1948.

Hanging on the Crosstrees

On Lake Erie
Off Madison, Ohio
Friday, November 10

William H. Thayer, the cook on the schooner *Juliette,* somehow commanded the strength to be the only survivor when his ship sank about three miles off Madison.

The *Juliette,* under command of Captain Albert Bassett, was bound from Vermillion, Ohio, to Kingston, Ontario, when it developed a leak. The crew worked at the pumps all afternoon, but the water gained. Bassett turned the vessel and made a run for Madison, hoping to reach the harbor before the boat sank. He didn't make it. The heavily laden ship foundered in thirty feet of water at 7:00 PM. It settled upright so the masts and crosstrees remained above water.

Thayer climbed to one of the crosstrees, and then hung there for nineteen hours before someone spotted him from shore and came out in a small boat to rescue him. Thayer said he didn't see any other members of the crew after the ship went down.

The *Juliette* was a new vessel, only two years old. It measured one hundred and fifty-four tons.

Bad Trip for the *Winslow*

On the St. Clair River
Port Huron, Michigan
Sunday, November 12

The propeller *Winslow* was making its way down the St. Clair River when the boat collided with the anchored schooners *Kate Hinchman* and *Traveler* at Port Huron. The thousand-ton steamship carried away the bow sprits and jib booms from both vessels, and took extensive damage to its own superstructure. A starboard cabin was demolished and the pilot house was shattered. The starboard anchor was lost. Nobody was hurt.

Captain McCrea said he could not avoid the accident. He said the *Winslow* steamed from Lake Huron into the river behind the slow moving tug *Brockway,* which was pulling a line of barges. The two anchored vessels blocked the river so the *Winslow* could not pass. McCrea said he ordered the engines slowed, but the steamer got caught in the current and drifted out of control into the two schooners.

The *Winslow's* trip, which began at Duluth, was marred with calamity. Before leaving Duluth harbor, the ship was caught in a gale, dragged her anchors, and ran aground.

Teeth of a New Storm

A new storm raged out of the northwest in mid-November, causing general havoc, especially on lakes Erie, Huron and Ontario. The blow started the night of Monday, November 13, and continued for the rest of the week.

The storm blew its worst on Lake Erie, where many boats were driven aground. Sailors died in the gale which was accompanied by snow and freezing rain.

That storm ushered in the first stage of severely cold winter weather which dominated the lakes through the end of November and most of December. The weather brought the shipping season to a close. Boats still on the lakes were caught by this and some even more dangerous storms that followed.

Saga of the *Gold Hunter*

On Georgian Bay
Monday, November 13

The schooner *Gold Hunter* had been stranded for a few days on a reef on Georgian Bay. It got pulled free by the Canadian gunboat *Prince Alfred* and the gunboat had it under tow, bound for Owen Sound, when the storm hit. Captain Frazer, commander of the gunboat, said the snow was so blinding and the gale so brutal that he believed his own boat was in danger and the *Gold Hunter* was certainly doomed. He said that when off Cabot's Head, he could not see the schooner and because of the strange way the vessel was pulling, he was convinced that it had capsized. He ordered the tow line cut to save his own ship.

The *Prince Alfred* arrived in port with five feet of water in the hold and its decks covered with a thick layer of ice. Newspapers reported the *Gold Hunter* lost with all hands. This wasn't the end of the story, however. Several days later it was learned that the schooner blew ashore in the storm and the crew of six sailors walked out of their ordeal alive.

The men said they launched a life boat and made it ashore at a remote place on Owen Sound. They were forty miles from the nearest house, so it took a while for them to walk out of the wilderness.

The *Gold Hunter* was built at Milford, Ontario, in 1862.

The Canadian gunboat *Prince Alfred* made an unsuccessful effort to save the schooner *Gold Hunter* in Georgian Bay.

Wreck of the *Twilight*

On Lake Huron
Wednesday, November 15

The three masted schooner *Twilight* damaged its rudder and put a hole in its hull when the boat hit a rock at 3:00 AM off Point aux Barques light. The gale was pounding the ship from the northwest so Captain Gibbs dropped anchors and battened down to ride out the storm.

His strategy didn't work. The anchors dragged and before the dawn came the *Twilight* was drifting off into deep water. The wind first blew the vessel southeast around the tip of Michigan's Thumb District. Then as if controlled by demon forces from below, the winds shifted to the north, just in time to push the ill-fated schooner south along the Michigan coastline, always within a few hundred feet of safety.

The sailors stuck by the ship as long as it remained afloat. At about 6:00 PM it was evident that the *Twilight* was sinking. Eight men abandoned ship in the yawl boat and rowed through the stormy seas for shore near Rock Falls. The surf overturned the frail craft and six of the eight sailors drowned.

The dead were identified as Gibbs, First Mate John Henwood, and sailors Charles Wilson, his brother William Wilson, Julius Williams and Alexander Rupert. Their bodies washed ashore the next day. Second Mate William Henwood, a brother to the first mate, and sailor William Rose reached shore alive.

The *Twilight* was on its way from Marquette to Erie with a cargo of iron ore. The schooner was built in Cleveland in 1862.

Wreck of the *Resolute*

On Lake Erie
Off Long Point
Wednesday, November 15

The gale was threatening to blow the brig *Resolute* off its course and to destruction on Long Point. The vessel was laden with paving stones on its way from Buffalo to Cleveland. The crew dropped anchors and tried to ride out the gale. The anchors dragged and the ship drifted ashore near the light. There the *Resolute* took a pounding and began to break up. The crew members saw that they could not survive aboard ship, and they started swimming for shore, clinging to pieces of the wreck. All but two made it. The ship's cook, Sarah Donahue, and seaman Robert W. Adams, froze to death. The *Resolute* was built in 1856 at Black River, Ohio.

The *P. C. Sherman* Disaster

On Long Point
Lake Erie
Wednesday, November 15

Capt. Charles McMillan told a board of inquiry that his decision to abandon the bark *P. C. Sherman* was made during the height of the storm because the ship's anchors were dragging and the hold was flooding. He said he was convinced that the boat would sink.

McMillan was under questioning because of the death of a member of his crew; an unidentified stewardess. People wanted to know why the woman was left by the other sailors to die in an open boat after it drifted ashore near Erie, Pennsylvania. The board also asked why the ship was abandoned at a time when it was still afloat and anchored off Long Point.

McMillan said circumstances prevented him or members of the *Sherman's* crew from doing anything to save the woman after the boat crashed on a rocky coast. His story was gripping. He said he quit the bark because he was concerned about the safety of his crew. Plans were to take the small boat to the Canadian shore and then hire a tug to save the ship. The captain didn't count on strong offshore winds that overpowered the oarsmen. The yawl with all of its occupants was blown away from shore and into the savage lake.

When the *Sherman* was found aground, tipped on its side and abandoned, it was assumed that the crew perished. First reports said all were probably lost. While people were recording them as lost, the crew was struggling for survival.

The sailors spent twenty terrifying hours in the open boat before the vessel was blown ashore at about 4:00 AM Thursday. By then, McMillan said everybody was numb from the cold and weak from the hours of exposure and going without food. A layer of ice covered their clothes and hair.

He said the little boat struck so hard against the rocks that oars were broken as the men tried to stave off the crash. Waves threatened to swamp the boat so it became every man for himself as the sailors scrambled on stiff, half frozen legs for the shore. The shore happened to be a very high bluff. The stewardess was too weak to save herself and the men lacked the strength to help her, McMillan said. He said it would have been difficult for anyone to have carried her up the bluff under normal circumstances. She was left behind in the boat to perish.

The *Sherman* was sailing from Chicago to Buffalo with twenty-five thousand bushels of corn.

Sinking of the *Eli Bates*

On Lake Erie
Off Ashtabula, Ohio
Wednesday, November 15

Nobody knows what happened aboard the schooner *Eli Bates* before it foundered with all hands. The *Bates,* under the command of twenty-six-year-old Capt. Timothy McEwen, sailed from Sheboygan, Wisconsin with a load of wheat bound for Buffalo. It never reached its destination. Sometime after the gale of November 15, the *Bates* was found resting upright on the bottom of Lake Erie, a few miles off Ashtabula. Its masts gave away the schooner's whereabouts because they were protruding out of the water.

It was rumored for a while that McEwen washed ashore, barely alive, lashed to a plank, but the story later turned out to be false. The other crew members included Mate Matthew Collins and Benjamin Dill.

Aboard the *Montcalm*

Off Long Point
Lake Erie
Wednesday, November 15

Another schooner making a last run of the season with a load of wheat that night was the *Montcalm,* under the command of Captain Tracy.

The *Montcalm* got in trouble earlier in the day when the cargo shifted. Tracy ordered the foresail jibed, then brought the ship on another tack to help put it upright again. He kept the boat running this way before the wind, even though he knew he was bringing it dangerously close to Long Point.

That afternoon a great wave struck the ship's stern, carrying away the yawl boat and causing a lot of damage. Shortly after that the *Montcalm* struck bottom and got hung up about five hundred feet off shore. Fortunately, the boat lay headed in, with the waves washing across the stern. If it had broached, the crew might have had to climb into the rigging to escape the seas and stay alive. As it was, the ship's stern cabin was flooded and the stove fire put out.

It was cold and uncomfortable, but all nine members of the crew . . . eight men and one woman . . . found shelter in the forecastle, where the upper bunks remained dry. They even had some food snatched from the galley. The crew lived this way for about two days before help arrived. The first attempt at rescue came the first day when sailors from the steamer *Michigan,* anchored nearby, launched a small boat. They were driven back. People on shore waited until the seas went down and then rigged up a mud scow on a rope system between the *Montcalm* and land. Several trips were made until all the sailors were transported to shore. They came two at a time.

The schooner **W. J. Webb** broke loose and went on a rampage during a storm at Cleveland.

Surviving the Gale in Cleveland Harbor

Cleveland, Ohio
Wednesday, November 15

The storm arrived at Cleveland at about 7:00 PM. It was described as a hurricane. The wind blew so hard the schooner *H. J. Webb,* lying at the coal docks, snapped a forward line and swung around, colliding with the nearby bark *Jennie P. Mack.* The *Webb's* bowsprit was broken and the *Mack* lost its top masts and rigging in the crash.

It was only the beginning of troubles as the storm intensified. The *Webb* was loose and on a rampage. The unmanned boat was driven by wind and waves across the river where it collided with the schooner *Fleetwing,* docked at the Railroad Bridge. The crash stove in the *Fleetwing's* bulwarks. In the meantime, the propeller *Passaic* broke away from its moorings and also drifted into the fleet causing extreme damage to the other ships anchored there.

Outside the harbor, the scow *H. G. Williams* was making a run for safety. The ship failed to clear the harbor entrance and struck the east pier. Captain Fuller ordered some of his men to jump on the pier and take a line, but they either ignored his command or failed to hear it in the storm. Fuller decided to take matters into his own hands. He jumped to the pier, but then failed to catch the line when the sailors tossed it to him. The wind was driving the scow down on the schooner *Grace Williams,* anchored just inside the harbor. Things were looking so desperate the crew abandoned ship. Two men jumped aboard the *Grace Williams* as the vessels hit, while two others tried to escape in a yawl boat. The yawl boat was swamped and the mate and cook of the *H. G. Williams* were drowned. The scow rolled over on its side, blocking the channel the next day.

Other Storm Casualties

The November 15 storm caused plenty of other trouble among the lakers. The other wrecks included:

➻ The schooner *George Foote* blew aground and broke up in Lake Ontario near Fort Niagara, Ontario. The crew escaped.

➻ The propeller *Evergreen City* was one of many vessels left wrecked on Lake Erie's Long Point. It was upbound with supplies for lumber camps at Au Sable when the storm overcame this steamer. The crew escaped. A salvage effort was made the next spring. The owners discovered that vandals had stripped the cabins of furnishings and even removed stained glass windows.

➻ The schooner *Alipeda,* Capt. Charles Hanscom, was on a trip from Buffalo to Toledo with two hundred and fifty tons of coal when it went ashore on the Lake Erie shore. The force of the waves drove the boat so far up on the beach the crew walked away, hardly getting wet.

➻ The Canadian bark *Rooney* went ashore three miles west of Fairport, Ontario. Ten sailors were rescued in an open boat brought from shore.

➻ The schooner *C. A. King* went aground at Long Point with twenty-two thousand bushels of wheat in the hold. When it investigated, the tug *Vulcan* found the crew still aboard, waiting for help. The *King* was pulled free and brought to Buffalo with little damage.

➻ The brig *Saxon,* a twenty-two-year lake veteran, also

got driven ashore on Long Point. The crew abandoned her, and before the storm was over, the boat was a total wreck.

➥The schooner *Theodore Perry* grounded on Long Point.

➥The propeller *Roanoke* was found anchored and disabled off Long Point the day after the storm. Its mast was carried overboard, the wheel was damaged and the rigging was tangled. Tugs towed the ship to Buffalo for repair.

➥The schooner *E. M. Porten* went ashore on Beaver Island, at the northern end of Lake Michigan. Later, when a tug pulled it off and took the boat in tow, the *Porten* sank in deep water about two miles offshore. The crew escaped in a life boat.

➥The propeller *J. L. Hurd* nearly foundered in the gale off Point aux Barques, Lake Huron. The ship got in a trough of the sea and was laid on its side for several anxious minutes before righting itself. The crew managed to get the *Hurd* turned again and the boat made it safely back to Port Huron.

➥The scow *Curlew* parted her tow line and was blown ashore near Port Hope, Michigan, on Lake Huron. The crew escaped.

➥The tug *W. B. Castle* was steaming upbound on Lake Huron with seven barges in tow when the storm developed. Five vessels broke loose. Three of them made it back to the St. Clair River, one dropped anchor at White Rock, and one was listed as missing.

➥The bark *James F. Joy* lost its foremast and headgear in the Straits of Mackinac and was discovered drifting in that condition by the steamer *Gordon Campbell*. The *Campbell* took the *Joy* in tow for awhile, but when the gale intensified, was forced to cut it loose again. The tug *Wilson* left Port Huron in search of the vessel. The *Joy* survived the storm because its registry continued until 1887, when the boat foundered on Lake Erie with a load of ore.

The bark *James F. Joy* got in trouble when caught in a bad storm on Lake Huron.

The *Illinois* Mystery

On Lake Michigan
Friday, November 17

Lake Michigan was still kicking up some angry rollers when the scow *Anna Tomine* came upon a floating, half submerged derelict about thirty miles off Milwaukee, Wisconsin. The wreck turned out to be the schooner *Illinois*, partly laden with heavy iron railroad ties, and barely afloat. The yawl boat was gone and it was assumed that the crew had abandoned the ship. Their fate was at first unknown. The *Tomine* took the wreck in tow and brought it into Milwaukee harbor around midnight.

The next day, people from all over town came down to look at the wreck and marvel that it still floated. The schooner's rudder, both anchors and hatches were gone, as well as the foresail and one jib. The interior of the cabin was wrecked, and the bulwarks on both sides were stove in nearly the complete length of the hull. On November 20, Captain S. C. Johnson showed up at Milwaukee to claim his ship. He said the *Illinois* was abandoned in the storm on the east side of the lake, off Michigan's Dean's Pier. After the schooner lost its rudder, the seas swept away the yawl boat, and an anchor was lost. Johnson said the ship was taking on water so fast the pumps couldn't keep up, and he believed the boat was sinking. He raised a distress signal and the crew was removed by a fishing boat.

Johnson said the *Illinois* had been taking on railroad ties at the time the storm developed. He said he cast off before the ship was fully loaded because the hull was pounding at the dock and he was afraid it would go to pieces.

That was Johnson's official story. A second version about how the *Illinois* went to sea without its crew was printed in the *Detroit Daily Post* on December 10. While the source of the story is not identified, the tale is worth re-telling. It goes like this:

The schooner *Illinois* went ashore south of Kewaunee, Wisconsin on Wednesday night and Captain Johnson decided to leave the crew in charge of the vessel while he went off to get help. When an offshore breeze came up, the crew decided to hoist sail, with the thought that the ship might work itself back into Lake Michigan. Nothing happened and the men got discouraged.

Later in the day, when their skipper didn't return, the entire crew decided to wade ashore and hike to the nearest town for beer and a warm meal. The sailors apparently weren't very smart or else they were very lazy. They didn't bother reefing the sails. While they were gone the tide came in and the wind freshened. Witnesses said the *Illinois* began moving off the bar and soon was sailing smartly off into Green Bay, with nobody aboard.

Whatever the truth, nobody could understand how the ship survived the storm and continued to float when the *Tomine* found it three days later.

Wreck of the *E. B. Allen*

On Thunder Bay
Lake Huron
Monday, November 20

A collision sank the schooner *E. B. Allen* on Monday night about six miles off the Thunder Bay light.

The *Allen,* downbound from Chicago to Buffalo with corn, was working its way against a southwesterly wind. The boat was close hauled on a starboard tack when it crossed the bow of the bark *Newsboy,* running north and free before the wind. The *Newsboy* slammed into the *Allen* amidships shortly after 10:00 PM. The schooner sank thirty minutes later.

The crew of the *Allen* escaped in the ship's yawl boat. The *Newsboy,* which had been sailing from Buffalo to Chicago, was badly damaged. It continued to float.

The *Jessie Anderson* Mystery

Off Long Point
Lake Erie
Friday, November 22

Nobody could explain why the schooner *Jessie Anderson* sank with all hands in relatively calm waters off Long Point. The *Anderson* took on fourteen thousand bushels of wheat at Port Colborne, Ontario, then set sail for Oswego, New York. The boat was towed down the river to Lake Erie by the tug *Urania,* then set off across Lake Erie never to be seen again.

The schooner *Melrose,* loaded grain at Port Colborne and left the following day, also bound for Oswego. The *Melrose's* skipper, Captain Lohr, said his vessel passed the masts of a sunken schooner. Because he was familiar with the *Anderson* he was able to identify the ship.

Among the lost crew members were Captain J. Ryan, Mate William Brown and a stewardess, Emily J. Philips. The others were unidentified.

The schooner wasn't located again until the summer of 1873, when the tug *W. A. Moore* found it in fifty-two feet of water, fifteen miles south southeast of Long Point. The *Anderson* was built in Sandusky, Ohio, in 1861.

Troubles on Lake Huron

On Lake Huron
Sunday, November 24

The problems began for the old sidewheel steamer *Huron* at 4:00 PM when she broke a cylinder off Lexington, Michigan. While floating disabled that evening, waiting for help, the *Huron* was struck by a passing schooner, the *Eliza Turner,* under tow behind the tug *Kate Moffat.*

The *Turner* rammed its bow into the port side of the disabled steamer, smashing side planks, rails and doing extensive damage. The impact toppled the *Turner's* masts and carried away the schooner's headgear.

Neither vessel sank. The *Huron* was towed into Port Huron by the steamer *Marine City.* Even though damaged, the nineteen-year-old steamer was repaired and put back in service. It operated another five years until it was abandoned at Grand Haven in the fall of 1877.

The steamer *Huron* was in a collision after it became disabled on Lake Huron.

Ice

As the onset of winter continued, stories were told about ship's sails and decks covered with ice, sailors having hands and feet frozen on the job, and vessels getting trapped in ice. Early in December the temperature dropped to an incredible 35 degrees below zero at Sault Ste. Marie, closing shipping on the canal earlier than usual and nearly freezing several ships on the St. Marys River. The temperature never got over five degrees during the entire month. The frigid cold threatened work on a coffer dam, which was needed for the construction of a new canal and lock. Workers managed to get the dam built, in spite of bad weather, but at great hardship.

Caught on Georgian Bay

At Byning Inlet
Georgian Bay
Sunday, November 26

The first incident of boats becoming trapped in ice happened when the lumber schooners *S. S. Robinson* and *San Jacinto* stayed too long at a mill on the north side of Byning Inlet .

When Captains James Bruce of the *Robinson* and B. S. Berry of the *San Jacinto* attempted to get away with their last load of the season bound for Chicago, they discovered their vessels fixed hard in six inches of ice. The crews, assisted by the men from the nearby mill, worked for three days, cutting and chopping a channel through the ice to the open water. After three days, and finding they had only moved the vessels about three-quarters of a mile, Bruce and Berry gave up and abandoned their boats for the winter. By then the ice was formed an estimated six miles from shore. The sails and rigging were stripped from the boats and everything was stored at the mill. The men also worked to get the tug *Minnie Hall* cut out of the ice and brought back into shelter at the mill.

131

The mate of the *San Jacinto* volunteered to stay with the ships and keep watch for the winter. Everybody else traveled by dog sleds, led by Indian guides, to Perry Sound about a hundred and twenty miles away. From there they traveled by team and walked another eighty-eight miles to Orilla, Ontario, where they got on a train for Toronto, and then went on to Buffalo. There were twenty-five travelers in the group, counting the two ship's crews and workers from the mill. They said the snow was twelve inches deep when they left the mill on December 2. The temperature was still plunging at well below zero, and it was storming almost every day.

The *Crosthwaite* Saga

On Saginaw Bay
Lake Huron
Tuesday, November 28

The ice build-up at the mouth of the Saginaw River blocked the grain loaded schooner *William Crosthwaite* from getting into Bay City harbor from Saginaw Bay. Captain Thomas Martin ordered the anchors dropped just offshore and announced that he would wait for conditions to improve. Thus began a twenty-two-day test of endurance that has few parallels in lake legend.

The weather remained cold and stormy. The *Crosthwaite* dragged its anchors and was pushed back out into the lake by moving ice. This continued until Friday, November 30, when the ship was about four miles from shore. There was a break in the weather on Saturday, and Martin ordered sail hoisted, and brought the *Crosthwaite* back in close to shore again only to find that the ice still blocked entrance to the harbor. Anchors were again dropped.

Again the movement of the ice caught the ship and carried it back into the lake. This time, the vessel was moved with the shifting ice past Point au Gres and finally past Charity Islands. Food ran low, so the crew was limited to only one meal a day. Fuel for the stoves ran out so the men began to break up the boat's superstructure to make firewood. Mean-

The Port Huron ferry *Sarnia* steamed out on Lake Huron to help the ice-bound schooner *Crosthwaite* into the harbor.

while, the owners of the *Crosthwaite* were getting worried. They announced on December 6 that they would pay a thousand dollars to any tug that could find the ship and bring it into port. The offer encouraged the crew of the tug *Coffin* to make a try, but the sailors couldn't get their vessel out of Bay City harbor.

On December 8, hunger and a fear of freezing to death drove the men of the *Crosthwaite* to make a daring attempt to escape to shore. First Mate A. H. Johnson lead a team of six other men on a dash across floating ice blocks. Together the sailors jumped from one shifting slab of ice to the next, carefully making their way toward shore. Two men fell through a crack in the ice and nearly drowned before they got pulled out again. After that it was all they could do to keep from freezing to death in their wet clothes. It was in this way that the seven, identified as Johnson, William Lee, Templar Fowler, William Kane, Michael Hasty, James Smith and Alexander Holyoke, made their way for eight miles to a deserted shore somewhere near Standish, Michigan. The seven spent the first night huddled together in an abandoned Indian hut before they reached Standish.

After that the problem was how to get food and fuel to Captain Martin and two other crew members, Second Mate John O'Brien and an unidentified woman cook, who would not leave the ship. R. L. Bradley, one of the ship's owners, and two other men, one of them identified as a Captain Burrington, made an unsuccessful try at carrying food and supplies across the ice from Sand Point. The project was abandoned after the *Crosthwaite* was found to be eight miles out in the lake, and moving about by the action of the wind and shifting ice. The team could not safely get close.

Bradley was in Detroit on December 15, trying again to hire a large tug to go out after the *Crosthwaite*. There were no takers. A few captains said they would go for a price, but their price was so outlandishly high, Bradley wouldn't pay it.

In the meantime, Captain Martin and his two-member crew continued to tear the ship apart for firewood. One day the ship got close to Charity Island and again lodged in solid ice. The men walked to the island and carried firewood and food supplies from the lighthouse keeper's stock back to the vessel. Martin prepared to spend the winter with his ship.

Then, late in the day on December 19, the weather broke and an offshore wind broke the schooner free. The three sailors hoisted sail and brought the *Crosthwaite* around the tip of the Thumb and sailed south, arriving at Port Huron the next day. People along the shore were amazed to see the schooner's sails. Word quickly spread to Port Huron that the *Crosthwaite* was free and on its way. The ferry steamer *Sarnia*, perhaps the only ship still operating and with steam up, went out on Lake Huron that afternoon to greet the long overdue schooner and tow it into port.

Aboard the *Antelope*

At Long Point
Lake Erie
Saturday, December 2

The schooner *Antelope* almost got trapped in the ice behind Long Point. Capt. H. Ballentine said he was bringing the ship from Buffalo to Detroit when he ran into heavy weather, was battling against northern winds, and ducked behind the point for shelter. The place turned out to be a not-so-pleasant haven because high seas were running and extreme cold set in. Chunks of broken ice were rubbing against the sides of the wooden hulled ship, threatening damage, and ice was building on the hull, especially across the bow, as each wave struck.

Ballentine said he began to worry that the ice was making the ship very heavy. He raised anchor and set sail back to Buffalo. The *Antelope* reached Buffalo harbor safely on Tuesday night, and Ballentine arranged to make winter quarters there.

Walking Away from the *Alice Craig*

On Lake Superior
Saturday, December 2

The schooner *Alice Craig* sailed from Duluth with supplies for Bayfield. The gale hit the *Craig* that night off Steamboat Island. Relentless seas thundered over the ship, carrying away the bowsprint, yawl and davits. Later the foresail was split and then the mainmast was broken away. The captain turned for Bark Point Bay, where he dropped anchor a mile offshore to ride out the blow.

The sub-zero cold moved in and by morning there was so much ice formed in the bay, the boat was locked in for the winter. The crew and passengers, including Major S. N. Clark, area Indian agent, and Capt. P. W. Smith, a second passenger, walked across the ice to shore.

Three Aground at St. Joseph

On Lake Michigan
At St. Joseph, Michigan
Sunday, December 3

The schooners *Industry* and *Active* and the scow *Dunham* were all driven ashore by the storm near St. Joseph, Michigan. The two schooners left St. Joseph at about the same time Sunday afternoon, got caught in the gale, and were shoved back to the shore a few hours later with thick layers of ice clinging to their decks. Peter Johnson of Sheboygan, Wisconsin, a passenger on the *Active,* was knocked overboard by a swinging boom and not seen again. The crew escaped but some had frozen toes and fingers.

The *Dunham* was sailing across the lake from Chicago when the storm hit. The boat was driven aground about four miles above St. Joseph. The captain scuttled her and the crew escaped.

Battling Intense Cold

On Lake Huron
Monday, December 4

The schooner *Lydia J. Rogers* was off Cove Island, Georgian Bay, when the extreme cold weather incapacitated her crew. The captain said the men were collapsing with frozen limbs and faces and could not remain on the deck or at the wheel for more than ten minutes at a time.

As the seas thundered over the deck, ice formed on everything. The windlass, anchors and chains were hidden under a blanket of ice. Axes had to be used to open the door to the forecastle.

The sailors rigged a spare sail at the bottom of one of the masts to give themselves shelter from the wind, but it was not enough. When the tug *Frank Moffat* hove in sight, the crew of the schooner welcomed her. The *Moffat* took the *Rogers* in tow to Port Huron, arriving Thursday afternoon. By then the ship was completely encased in ice.

On the *Board of Trade*

On Lake Michigan
Tuesday, December 5

The bark *Board of Trade* was among the fleet of boats attempting to make one final trip that fateful week. It left Chicago with a load of corn only hours before getting caught in the storm on lower Lake Michigan. The ship was buffeted by wet, freezing snow and heavy seas at first. Later the wind blew intense cold and the spray from the seas began icing the decks and rigging. The sailors found themselves in a battle for their lives. The ropes and pulleys froze so hard the sails could not be taken in from the deck. When men were sent aloft to pull in the stiff canvas one sailor was overcome at his post. He had to be lowered to the deck with ropes where his mates rubbed him with snow until he was revived. The sailors all suffered frostbite.

Ice formed so quickly that there was fear the ship would sink or capsize from the extra weight. The captain turned the ship around and ran with the wind for Chicago. The snowfall was so thick that visibility dropped to zero. The captain and mate took turns climbing aloft to see what was ahead. Several times they were so numb with cold they also had to be rubbed with snow. At last the lights of Calumet were seen. The ship dropped anchor until the tug *Crawford* brought her into port the next day.

Saving the *Lake Forest*

On Lake Erie
Off Erie, Pennsylvania
Tuesday, December 5

The schooner *Lake Forest* dropped anchor just outside the breakwater at Erie during the storm. The boat was on the last leg of a trip from Chicago to Buffalo with a load of corn. The vessel was noticed by people in Erie the next morning while the storm was still raging. Nobody volunteered to take a tug through the storm and into the building ice field to reach the schooner, even though the vessel was obviously in trouble. Waves could be seen dashing wildly over the ship's ice-laden decks, and some said she was down by the head.

Later in the day, the iron steamer *China* fired up its boilers and the crew made plans to rescue the *Lake Forest*. The steamer either failed to batter a way through the ice, or the captain changed his mind. The *China* never left port. On Thursday, a group of volunteers walked across the ice, with the help of an open boat, and succeeded in getting close enough

The schooner *Lake Forest* survived the storm at Erie. The crew stayed with the boat to save it.

to talk to the seven sailors aboard the ship. It was learned that the crew had only two more days of food. The *Lake Forest's* sails were wrecked, its main mast was broken off, and the decks were slicked with ice. There was no life boat aboard. Even though things were bad, the crew declined help in getting ashore. The sailors said they wanted to stay and try to save their ship. Food was brought out and the schooner *Harrison* donated a life boat.

The storm continued to blow hard the rest of the week. On Friday, conditions got so bad the ship's anchor chain parted and it was feared that the *Lake Forest* would be smashed in the ice. The crew dropped a second anchor and it held. The hardships experienced by those sailors that week were known only to themselves. Finally on Tuesday, December 12, the weather calmed enough for the tugs *Perew* and *Bryand* to get a line to the schooner and pull it east to Buffalo. She reached port safely the next day.

The *Guido*

On Lake Michigan
Wednesday, December 6

The two-masted schooner *Guido* was battling its way through the tempest toward Milwaukee. The ship was in bad shape. Its sails were ripped by the wind and much of the rigging was torn away. Even though the lights of the city were in sight, the experienced sailors did not have enough sail left to work the *Guido* into Milwaukee harbor.

Carried by northwesterly winds, the schooner was blown back across the lake to the Michigan coast, where it put in at Grand Haven. The crew came ashore, many of the men suffering from frost bite and exposure. One man was struck in the face by a flying jib sail and some thought he might lose an eye. The food ran out and the men were weak from hunger.

The *Guido* survived the storm to become one of the oldest working sailing ships in lakes history. It was built at Manitowoc, Wisconsin, in 1856 and was not dropped from registration until 1939, eighty-three years later.

Schooner *Guido* passing through Taylor Street Bridge, Chicago, 1900.

SUMMING UP

A Dangerous Profession

Being a sailor on the Great Lakes was risky in 1871. Anyone employed on the boats worked long, hard hours aboard frail craft that had a high chance of being wrecked or sunk. They were exposed to high pressure steam engines that sometimes exploded, and climbed rigging in sailing ships that occasionally tossed them into the sea to drown. They worked aboard wooden ships that caught fire, went aground, broke up and sank in severe storms. They did it for wages that ranged from a dollar to a dollar and seventy-five cents a day, depending on the company they worked for or the business climate of the season.

Sailors lived in deplorable conditions, on leaking, tumbling boats. They bunked together in forecastles where each man had a small locker in which to keep his worldly possessions. There was no family life. The best that each man could hope for was a place to sleep and three meals a day from the ship's galley. Yet people were drawn to this life for unexplainable reasons. They came even though their attraction to ships and the sea occasionally brought them to horrible and painful death. Some examples of how sailors were hurt or killed in 1871:

↝On March 22, engineer George Smith and two unknown firemen were badly scalded when a steam pipe they were working on blew away from the side of a boiler on the propeller *Lake Breeze*. The ship was docked at Bay City and Smith was getting the engines ready for the season.

⇥Frank Murray, Detroit, first mate on the schooner *Plover,* was knocked overboard and drowned off the head of Lake Huron's Presque Isle on April 10. Murray had been working on the tackle to the main boom when the accident happened at 2:30 AM. The captain heard his cry and turned the ship around. A lifeboat was launched and sailors spent several hours in the dark searching the waters. No trace of Murray was found. The water was so cold at that time of year that even if he could swim, Murray probably died from hypothermia within a few minutes.

⇥Captain Hurst, master of the schooner *Union Jack,* of Kingston, Ontario, was knocked overboard by a swinging main boom on the night of July 23. He disappeared somewhere in Lake Huron and was never seen again.

⇥Seaman John Allen drowned after he fell from a yawl boat while it was being hoisted into the davits on the schooner *G. D. Russell*. The accident happened on Saginaw Bay on July 22.

⇥An unknown sailor toppled over the side of the bark *Champion* while he was leaning over to wash the side of the ship. By the time the vessel was turned around, the man disappeared beneath the waves. The accident happened on Lake Michigan on about August 3.

⇥Sailor Thomas Shaw, Toledo, was knocked overboard by a swinging boom from the scow *Rough and Ready* and was drowned in Lake Erie on August 11.

⇥Minnie Berthwick, cook for the schooner *Skylark,* fell overboard and drowned off Port Stanley, Ontario, sometime in August.

⇥Sailor John Doran of Cleveland fell from a lifeboat on the bark *Superior,* as it hung from the davits, and drowned on the Detroit River. The accident happened August 28.

Adding Up the Year

When it was over, a government official at Detroit issued the following statistics for marine disasters, shipwrecks and troubles for the year 1871.

There were one thousand, one hundred and sixty-seven vessels in some kind of difficulty on all of the Great Lakes. Of these, two hundred twenty-five were involved in collision, two hundred eighty ships were driven ashore, thirty-one burned, twenty-six capsized, nineteen foundered, one hundred thirty-two sprang leaks, sixty-five waterlogged, sixty were demasted, one hundred ten lost deck loads and ten boilers exploded.

There were two hundred and seventy-two deaths among sailors. Of these, two hundred and fourteen were drowned, twenty-six died by falling or other miscellaneous accidents aboard ship, three were murdered, and the rest committed suicide or died of natural causes. Obviously, not all were reported in this book.

It was feared that the terrible fire that leveled Chicago early in October would have a long range impact on the Great Lakes shipping industry, but that was not the case. Even though the fire destroyed six elevators containing one and a half million bushels of grain, it was only a temporary set-back. New elevators were built and grain shipments continued to arrive, if only to be stored on the open ground until ships could haul them away. By year's end, Chicago grain dealers reported handling a record eighty-three and a half million bushels of grain and flour, passing a previous record of slightly more than sixty-nine and a half million bushels received in 1868.

The number of hogs packed during 1871 at Chicago totaled over a million, compared to eight hundred fifty-six thousand the year before. Business prospects seemed to be growing faster than Chicago could rebuild.

Notes by the Author

The research behind this book started in 1984 when, as a bureau reporter for *The Times Herald,* a Port Huron, Michigan daily newspaper, I began writing stories about Huron County's quest to mark a large area of Lake Huron coastline as an underwater preserve. The State of Michigan allows a certain number of acres of lake bottomland along its coasts to be protected preserves, where it is illegal to tamper with or remove items from shipwrecks found there.

Marking the area as a preserve signaled to sports divers that it is a good place to explore shipwrecks, which in turn is good for the local economy which feeds on tourism. I am a historian but not a diver so I received completely different signals from the news. I woke up to the fact that we had a raw, untapped source of Great Lakes history lying within a few hundred feet of our own back yard.

To get their preserve, Huron County authorities declared a probable list of about a hundred wrecks believed lying along the shore between Port Austin and Harbor Beach, mostly in the area of Pointe aux Barques at the tip of the little peninsula known as Michigan's Thumb Area. No more than a dozen of these wrecks had been found.

When I got my hands on that list and some of the possible dates when these vessels sank, I was compelled to start digging through the microfilm files of my newspaper in search of the stories behind the wrecks. What I found was exciting! Not only did the stories about the wrecks pop up, but I discovered hundreds of other exciting stories about shipwrecks that happened all over Lakes Huron, Superior, Michigan, Erie and Ontario. My quest soon led me to the Detroit Public Library, and then on to the Institute for Great Lakes Research, a storehouse of data, books, records, blueprints and photographs of nearly everything known about ships and shipping on the

Great Lakes. After uncovering hundreds of great stories, I began looking around for a way to pass them on to others in the way I enjoy best, the printed page. It is my nature to tell a good yarn when I find it, and these were just too good to let go untold. I began writing a weekly column, which appears in *The Times Herald, Marquette Mining Journal,* the *Huron Daily Tribune,* Bad Axe, and in a summer recreation magazine published by *The Record Eagle* at Traverse City, Michigan.

I also began planning a book.

The problem was choosing a topic. Other writers already published wonderful stories about the best known wrecks in a long string of books that can be found in most libraries and book stores in the Midwest. I wanted to do something different. I would present a slice of history . . . possibly from one specific era . . . so readers could understand the shipping industry for that period. I wanted to include a glimpse of how sailors lived and died, and tell the frequency of disasters aboard ships in the early days of sail and steam.

With this thought in mind, I began research for a collection of short stories about events on the lakes between 1871 and 1880. For some reason I didn't start with 1871. I first collected data from 1875 and 1876, and was amazed at the large amount of information I had. It was not long before I realized that an entire book could be written about any one of these dramatic years. Next I zeroed in on 1871 because this year brought some serious shipwrecks, the Chicago fire and great forest fires that swept Wisconsin and Michigan. It also was a year of information that was harder to get. I had to travel farther to read the microfilm files and search harder to get the complete stories.

Even though government documents can be found from 1871, I discovered that the best source of information from this historical period was newspaper microfilm files. There were problems. Newspapers in that period mostly existed to promote one political interest or another. Major news events of the day seemed to be tacked on the last page as an afterthought, once the important political news and advertising got the space it needed. Only a few newspapers along the coast took an interest in what was happening on the lakes. When stories were found, I realized that the writers had a tendency to be careless about names and facts. Names sometimes were spelled several different ways. Sometimes editors assumed that since most people in town already knew all of the facts, or perhaps a competitive newspaper (not saved on microfilm) had already printed them, they didn't need to repeat this information. A story might only tell new information, without ever going back to explain the original event.

Stories sometimes included rumors that later proved to be false. A second account, sometimes found in another newspaper, might correct the error, or simply repeat it. Newspapers in 1871 almost never corrected their own mistakes.

Getting captain's names was a serious problem. Editors had a tendency to refer to the master of a ship as "Captain Smith" or "Captain Jones" without ever printing his first name. Sometimes we got around that by tracking the name in records of the *Board of Supervising Inspectors of Steam Vessels,* or going to biographies found in Beer's *History of the Great Lakes.* This was tricky because there were many lakes pilots with the same last name operating at the same time, and it was important to connect a specific man with the ship we were writing about. When all else failed, I simply used the captain's last name for this record. I sought accuracy, although I must admit, there is data in this book that can only be supported from news clippings of the day. If they were wrong, the historic record may forever be wrong.

Many of the stories are extremely brief. That is because nothing more could be learned. Yet the hours of detective work that went into them might surprise you. The little story of the wreck of the *P. C. Sherman* off Long Point on November 15 is just one example of the frustrations involved in tracking down what appeared to be a fine story of the sea. Most newspapers of the day listed the *Sherman* as one of several wrecks on Lake Erie during that storm. Beers *History of the Great Lakes* is among them. All of the accounts agreed that the crew was lost with the ship. One day while digging through old news clips from the files at Perrysburg, I came upon a fragment of a clipping from the *Erie Daily Dispatch* which hinted that there were survivors from the *Sherman.* The story was titled "Terrible Voyage in an Open Boat," and indicated that it would contain the personal account of one of the survivors. Unfortunately, the story was missing.

Newspapers in that day liked to copy good yarns like that, so I began searching for the same story in other papers. The only other account appeared in the November 23 issue of the *Detroit Free Press*. The microfilm photographer, however, did such a sloppy job that the story was blurred and could not be read. Then I found a clipping in the *Detroit Daily Post* that said nearly all of the crew members arrived at Buffalo after spending twenty hours drifting across Lake Erie in an open boat. There was one death. The story said a woman, identified only as the stewardess, died from exposure. Finally, I found a story in the *Buffalo Express* about the captain defending his decision to abandon the *Sherman,* and explaining just how the woman died. The story did not name the woman or give much detail about the events that happened in the open boat. It was enough information to make a story, however. I never did find that first hand account.

This book does not include every shipwreck story on the Great Lakes in 1871. For example, I could not find any information about an explosion aboard the tug *General Lyon* at Sandusky, Ohio, the fire that claimed the steamer *Iroquois,* or the burning of the steamer *Victoria* on Lake Ontario. I have a list of about a half dozen other vessels that either foundered or went ashore that year, but dates, places or details of the wrecks could not be confirmed. Perhaps I gave up too early. If this is so, please accept my apologies.

James L. Donahue

Nautical Terms:

Aft: The rear, or stern end of a ship.

Barge: A roomy, sometimes flat-bottomed ship designed to transport bulk cargo. It can move under sail, be towed, or be powered by an engine.

Bark: A three-masted sailing ship with foremast and mainmast square rigged, and mizzenmast fore-and-aft rigged.

Barkentine: A three-masted sailing ship with foremast square rigged and the other two masts fore-and-aft rigged.

Bow: The front or forward end of a ship.

Buoy: a floating marker anchored in water to show locations of channels or sunken obstacles.

Fore-and-aft: In reference to sails of a ship, the canvass runs in the general line of the length of the vessel. Also located in, at or toward both the bow and stern of the ship.

Hawser: A thick rope or cable used in pulling or mooring a ship.

Lighter: A large, flat bottomed boat or scow used to unload cargo from ships not able to tie up at wharves.

Propeller: A vessel driven through the water by propellers instead of side wheels. The ship can be powered by either steam or diesel engines.

Port: The left side of a ship to a person on the deck and looking forward toward the bow.

Reef: A chain of rocks or sand lying near the surface of the water. Also used as a verb which means reducing the amount of working canvas on a sailing ship.

Rigging: The ropes and pulleys that support and control a ship's sails, masts and spars.

Schooner: A sailing ship with fore and aft rigging. Most schooners have two masts but larger vessels can have three, four and even rarely, five masts.

Scow: A large flat-bottomed boat with broad, square ends.

Sidewheeler: a steam powered vessel propelled through the water by large paddle wheels mounted on both sides.

Starboard: The right side of a ship to a person standing on the deck and looking forward toward the bow.

Steamboat, steamer or steamship: Any vessel powered by a steam engine. In old accounts, most commonly used for ships propelled by side mounted paddle wheels.

Stern: The rear, or aft end of a ship.

Superstructure: The cabins, pilot house and other buildings above the main deck of a ship.

Tug or tugboat: A ship with powerful engines designed for towing.

Waterlogged: The condition of a wooden ship in a sinking condition, but buoyed up by a cargo of material that is lighter than water.

Wharf: A dock or pier used in loading or unloading ships.

Yawl: a lifeboat on a ship.

Bibliography

Beers, J. H. and Co., *History of the Great Lakes with Illustrations,* Volumes 1 and 2, Chicago, 1899.

Board of Supervising Inspectors of Steam-Vessels, proceedings of the Twentieth Annual Meeting held at Washington, D. C., January, 1872; Washington Government Printing office, 1872.

Buffalo Courier, 1871 editions, Buffalo Public Library, Buffalo, N.Y.

Buffalo Express, 1871 editions, Buffalo Public Library, Buffalo, N.Y.

Cleveland Daily Leader, 1871 editions, Cleveland Public Library microfilm file, Cleveland, Ohio.

Cleveland Herald, 1871 editions, Cleveland Public Library microfilm file, Cleveland, Ohio.

Cleveland Plain Dealer, 1871 editions, Cleveland Public Library microfilm file, Cleveland, Ohio.

Detroit Free Press, 1871 editions, Detroit Public Library microfilm file, Detroit, Mich.

Detroit Daily Post, 1871 editions, Michigan State Library microfilm file, Lansing, Mich.

Detroit Tribune, 1871 editions, Detroit Public Library microfilm file, Detroit, Mich.

Erie Daily Dispatch, 1871 editions, Erie Public Library microfilm file, Erie, Pa.

Erie Observer, 1871 editions, Erie Public Library microfilm file, Erie, Pa.

Institute for Great Lakes Research, news clipping files and other data, division of Bowling Green University, Perrysburg, Ohio.

Manistee Times, 1871 editions, Michigan State Library microfilm file, Lansing Mich.

Muskegon Enterprise, 1871 editions, Michigan State Library microfilm file, Lansing, Mich.

News and Reporter, Muskegon, Mich., 1871 editions, Michigan State Library microfilm file, Lansing, Mich.

Port Huron Weekly and *Daily Times,* 1871 editions, Port Huron Public Library microfilm file, Port Huron, Mich.

St. Joseph Herald, St. Joseph, Mich., 1871 editions, Michigan State Library microfilm file, Lansing, Mich.

Saugatuck Lake Shore Commercial, 1871 editions, Michigan State Library microfilm file, Lansing, Mich.

Tri-Weekly Journal, Bay City, 1871 editions, Michigan State Library microfilm files, Lansing, Mich.

Illustrations

Barber, J., prop., page 51. Photo courtesy Institute for Great Lakes Research, Perrysburg, Ohio.

Bay City, str. barge, page 25. Photo courtesy Institute for Great Lakes Research, Perrysburg, Ohio.

Butcher Boy, sch., page 83. Photo courtesy Institute for Great Lakes Research, Perrysburg, Ohio.

Coburn, R. G., prop., page 94 and page 97. Photos courtesy Great Lakes Marine Historical Collection, Milwaukee Public Library, Milwaukee, Wis.

Couch, James, sch., appears as *Tasmania,* page 8. Photo courtesy Institute for Great Lakes Research, Perrysburg, Ohio.

Favorite, prop., page 86. Photo courtesy Institute for Great Lakes Research, Perrysburg, Ohio.

Forester, str., dock scene, page 31. Photo courtesy Institute for Great Lakes Research, Perrysburg, Ohio.

Gould, Jay, prop., page 71. Photo courtesy Institute for Great Lakes Research, Perrysburg, Ohio.

Guido, sch., page 139. Photo courtesy Institute for Great Lakes Research, Perrysburg, Ohio.

Hackett, R. J., str. barge, page 37. Photo courtesy Institute for Great Lakes Research, Perrysburg, Ohio.

Huron, str., page 130. Photo courtesy Institute for Great Lakes Research, Perrysburg, Ohio.

India, prop., page 116. Photo courtesy Institute for Great Lakes Research, Perrysburg, Ohio.

Joy, James F., bark, page 127. Photo of painting, courtesy Institute for Great Lakes Research, Perrysburg, Ohio.

Lake Forest, sch., page 138. Photo courtesy Great Lakes Marine Historical Collection, Milwaukee Public Library, Milwaukee, Wis.

La Petite, sch., page 103. Photo courtesy Institute for Great Lakes Research, Perrysburg, Ohio.

Logan, Eliza, sch., page 109. Photo courtesy Institute for Great Lakes Research, Perrysburg, Ohio.

Maine, prop., page 46. Photo courtesy Institute for Great Lakes Research, Perrysburg, Ohio.

Marine City, sidewheel steamer, page 15. Photo courtesy Institute for Great Lakes Research, Perrysburg, Ohio.

Mason, R. P., sch., page 101. Photo courtesy Institute for Great Lakes Research, Perrysburg, Ohio.

McClellan, George B., tug, page 113. Artist's drawing courtesy Great Lakes Marine Historical Collection, Milwaukee Public

Library, Milwaukee, Wis.

Index of Ships

Golden Fleece, sch., aground at Port Austin Reef, pg. 54.
Golden Harvest, collision at Straits of Mackinaw, pg. 39.
Gold Hunter, sch., wrecked on G. Bay, pg. 118.
Goodnow, tug, operating on L. Huron, pg. 109.
Gould, Jay, str., in collision at S. Manitou Is., pg. 71.
Graves, W. T., str. bg., on lakes, pg 18.
Guido, sch., survived gale on L. Mich., pg. 139.

H

Hackett, R. J., str. barge, stuck at St. Clair Flats, pg. 37.
Hall, Minnie, tug, caught in ice, G. Bay, pg. 131.
Harrison, sch., operating at Erie, pg. 138.
Harvest Home, collision on L. Erie, pg. 79.
Helfenstein, brig, operating on L. Erie, pg. 63.
Hinchman, Kate, sch., collision on St. Clair River, pg. 117.
Homer, bark, grounded at flats, pg. 37
Hotchkiss, barge, operating on L. Erie, pg. 112.
Hurd, C. H., sch., foundered in L. Mich., one saved, pg. 73.
Hurd, J. L., prop., nearly foundered on L. Huron, pg. 126.
Huron, str., helped Mich. fire victims, pg. 84; broke down
off Lexington, L. Huron, pg. 130.
Hurt, str., operating on L. Erie, pg. 63.

I

Illinois, sch., found abandoned on L. Mich., pg. 127.
Imperial, sch., collision on L. Huron, pg. 106.
India, prop., sunk on L. George, pg. 115.
Industry, sch., aground at St. Joseph, L. Mich., pg. 135.
Islander, tug, operating at Straits of Mackinaw, pg. 62.

J

Japan, prop., grounded Fighting Is., Detroit River, pg. 106.
Jerome, George, str., collision on Detroit River, pg. 73.
Jessie, sch., collision at Straits, pg. 61
Jessie, tug, lost rudder on Detroit River, pg. 66.
Johnson, Andrew, U. S. revenue cutter, pg. 115
Johnston, Hattie, sch., collision L. Huron, pg. 78.
Jones, B. B., tug, exploded at Port Huron, pg. 34.
Joy, James F., bark, nearly lost on L. Huron, pg. 126.
Juliette, sch., foundered on L. Erie, pg. 117.

K

King, C. A., sch., on Long Point, L. Erie, pg. 125.
King, James C., bark, collision L. Huron, pg. 24.

Y

Young, Annie, prop., rescue on L. Erie, pg. 63; aground on Detroit River, pg. 65.

Z

Zonave, tug, towing lumber barges on L. Erie, pg. 58.

About The Author

James L. Donahue was born June 1, 1938 at Harbor Beach, Michigan. He discovered an interest in writing in high school and took a part-time job on the *Harbor Beach Times*. While in college, Donahue took a year off from his studies to work for the *Huron Daily Tribune,* Bad Axe, Michigan. Following graduation from Central Michigan University with majors in Journalism and English literature, Donahue went to work for the former *News-Palladium* in Benton Harbor, Michigan, worked two years at the *Kalamazoo Gazette,* Kalamazoo, Michigan, and finally became Sanilac County bureau chief for the *Times Herald*, Port Huron, Michigan, in 1971. He retired in 1993 to found Anchor Publications, a family-owned publishing business involved in literary and historical writing and research.

Donahue writes a syndicated weekly column for the *Times Herald,* the *Mining Journal,* Marquette, Mich., and the *Huron Daily Tribune,* Bad Axe, Mich., about shipwrecks and other historical events on the lakes. His stories also have appeared in the *Grand Rapids Press* and the *Traverse City Record Eagle.* In 1991, Donahue included seventy-five of his best stories in a collection titled *Terrifying Steamboat Stories,* published by Altwerger & Mandel Publishing Co.

His latest books, *Schooners in Peril and Steamboats In Ice 1872* were both produced by Anchor Publications of Cass City in 1995. Both books deal with shipwrecks on the Great Lakes.

Donahue collaborated with Judge James H. Lincoln of Harbor Beach in the book *Fiery Trial,* a historical account of a forest fire that swept the Thumb Area of Michigan in 1881. *Fiery Trial* was published by the Historical Society of Michigan in 1984. Anchor Publications reprinted a revised form of *Fiery Trial,* with the cooperation of the Historical Society, in 1994.

In 1982, Donahue and his wife, Doris, owned and used an old-time wood-burning cook stove in their home. They wrote and published *Cooking On Iron*, a collection of early American recipes ranging from Chestnut Soup and Hickory Nut Cake, to making soap. His story, *The Day We Wrecked the Train*, a personal account about growing up at Harbor Beach, appeared in a special edition of *Good Old Days Magazine* in 1987.

James and Doris Donahue formerly lived near Cass City, Mich., with their daughter, Jennifer. The Donahues, who now reside in Arizona, have three other children; Aaron, who lives with his wife, Gayle, in California, Ayn Bishop, of Georgia, and Susie Donahue, who lives in Germany.